Items should be returned on or before the last date
shown below. Items not already requested by other
borrowers may be renewed in person, in writing or by
telephone. To renew, please quote the number on the
barcode label. To renew online a PIN is required.
This can be requested at your local library.
Renew online @ **www.dublincitypubliclibraries.ie**
Fines charged for overdue items will include postage
incurred in recovery. Damage to or loss of items will
be charged to the borrower.

**Leabharlanna Poiblí Chathair Bhaile Átha Cliath
Dublin City Public Libraries**

Baile Átha Cliath
Dublin City

Date Due	Date Due	Date Due
18 JUN 2018	03 APR 2018	08 APR 2018
	08 JAN 2020	

Dedication

To Ciara and Darragh, the source of my inspiration and great love.

To my family and friends, for the blanket of love and support they have woven around me.

To those of you who need a little light to shine in the darkness, to remind you that you are not alone. I hope my story can provide some comfort.

SEE YOU IN TWO MINUTES, MA

"A powerful and moving testimony to an unbearable grief"
PAULA MEEHAN

LINDA ALLEN

DARCIAR BOOKS

First published in 2016 by
Darciar Books
Kildare, Ireland
www.lindaallen.ie

Paperback	ISBN: 978-1-911013-341
Ebook – Mobi format	ISBN: 978-1-911013-358
Ebook – epub format	ISBN: 978-1-911013-365
CreateSpace	ISBN: 978-1-911013-372

Produced by Kazoo Independent Publishing Services
222 Beech Park, Lucan, Co. Dublin
www.kazoopublishing.com

Kazoo Independent Publishing Services is not the publisher of this work. All rights and responsibilities pertaining to this work remain with Darciar Books.

Kazoo offers independent authors a full range of publishing services. For further details visit www.kazoopublishing.com

Cover design by Andrew Brown
Printed in the EU

About the author

L
inda Allen worked as a Montessori and special education teacher before training to become a therapist. She specialises in a range of therapies, including intuitive counselling, polarity therapy, reiki and cellular healing. She has worked for the Health Service Executive as an access worker in child protection cases and as a personal growth and development tutor for the Education and Training Boards. In private practice, she works with individuals and groups in the areas of personal empowerment, stress resilience and life skills. She also acts as a celebrant of civil marriages and other family occasions. She lives in Sallins, County Kildare, with her partner, Derek.

Acknowledgements

This book exists because of the support and contributions of so many people. Words cannot express my gratitude, but I want to offer my heartfelt thanks to the following:

To Dr Johnny Connolly for his unwavering belief, support and dedication to bringing my story to light. As well as his practical input, his energy and enthusiasm encouraged me and propelled this project forward. If it wasn't for him, these words might still be in a journal. I am deeply indebted.

To my loving family: my daughter, Ciara, my parents, Eileen and Dermot, and my siblings, Gregg, Louise and Ken, who each in their own unique way provided me with strength and sustenance amidst their own loss. I am grateful for you every day.

To my partner, Derek, and my inner circle and close friends. You know who you are and how precious you are to me. You have been the cornerstone of my renewal. I am astounded by your caring support, creativity and thoughtfulness.

To Darragh's crew, the wonderful teenagers – now young adults – for your capacity to help and support one another in incredibly difficult circumstances. Your sensitivity continually surprises and delights me.

To poet and writer Paula Meehan for your endorsement of my words and your genuine interest in birthing this book.

To the bands who performed at my fundraisers for the love of music and as a tribute to Darragh and our family: Savage Jim Breen and Proudfoot in Whelan's, Shaun Doyle, The Valentine Blacks, The Spirit Merchants, The Sneas and Bunoscionn in Monasterevin Pavilion.

To the community of Rathangan, especially the youth club and its leaders, for reaching out to us and meeting our unusual request to hold Darragh's funeral at the community centre and for the support and services they offer to the young people of the town.

To the anonymous caretaker who consistently tends to Darragh's place of rest.

To Dave and Sinéad, who are navigating their own path through grief, and the ray of sunshine, Darragh's brother, Cillian.

To the staff and students in VTOS, Athy. Your kindness and sensitive support was outstanding.

To graphic designer Marguerite McEntee for a wonderful job on my website and for being so full of ideas and easy to work with.

To all those on the road to self-discovery who have shared moments of pain and love during workshops both here and in Thailand, especially with Don and Jen Hanson and Transforming Cellular Memory.

To Fund It, a wonderful crowd-funding organisation run by a dedicated, professional and approachable team – Andrew Hetherington, Orla Basquille and Claire Fitzgerald.

To all those who pledged their support to my book – family, those I know and love, friends of friends and anonymous strangers who put their faith in my writing.

To John and Ena Kennedy for their support.

To the team at Kazoo for the professional, friendly service that made the road to self-publishing a pleasant experience. To Chenile Keogh, for managing the process, Maria McGuinness and Robert Doran for editing, and Andrew and Rebecca Brown for the cover.

To all of you who shared your personal stories of your turmoil, trials and struggles, and to those walking the path of recovery from grief, especially through suicide.

Chapter 1
'See you in two minutes, Ma!'

'See you in two minutes, Ma!' The words echoed in the hallway as the front door closed then burst open again, followed by the quick trundling of long legs up and down the stairs. All over in a blur. This time silence remained, uninterrupted. I was standing in the kitchen ironing some innocuous piece of clothing, on an ordinary Saturday evening, in an ordinary house, in a normal cul-de-sac with a grassy area where children kick ball and have tea parties with plastic tea sets; where he and his crew camp out; where they wrestle with each other, take selfies, plan battles on Xbox, dance, sing, shout and share a smoke behind a wall. Here in this ordinary life, the unthinkable happened. My life was transformed forever that evening. It was the last time I saw him alive.

That scene plays over and over in my mind, etched forever in my memory, as I examine those last moments with forensic determination, looking for a clue, an indication, a something. There has got to be a something that could have, would have, changed the outcome. What did I miss? But like a scratch on an old vinyl record, the needle returns to the same thought processes, the outcome remains unchanged – he's no longer here. He left us by his own hand, his own choice. My mind is screaming so many words but the truth is unwavering. He is fifteen years old. He is supposed to be here! But Darragh is gone. All over in a blur!

And so my life stopped and began again as the mother of a suicide victim. Those words sit uncomfortably in the air. What was he a victim of? Love? Teenage angst? Depression? Are these the words associated with him now and forever more to try to make sense of this event? His absence means there is no defence. People can make up their own minds about what ailed him.

But – but – but – he was the life and soul of the party, the glue that held his crew together, the laughter, the joker, the music maker, the risk taker. He bustled in and out of the door always accompanied by mates. He danced around the kitchen, opening and shutting the cupboard doors looking for food that stared back at him from laden shelves as he declared there was nothing to eat. Boisterous in his enthusiasm for music and socialising, loving his friends in a deeply loyal way, things were never quiet in his wake. He was mature in so many ways as his body grew and changed overnight into a manly composition – hairy legs in training shorts, a shadow over his lip. Hair gel and deodorant became prized possessions and it was almost a crisis if either were in short supply. Such a paradox of emotions emanated from him – such a typical teenager.

Boundaries were made to be tested and that's exactly what he did. And so, when two minutes didn't return him home I didn't think too much of it. Gone for a smoke, I thought discontentedly. Yes, I knew he smoked, and he knew I knew because he told me himself. He told me a lot of the things he and his friends did – hardly the typical profile of a young man contemplating suicide. In fact, he had been at a party the night before and he was to fill me in on the details on the way to his father's. I liked those short trips to and from his father's. The car was a space where, uninterrupted, we could really connect. Of course during some trips he sat with his earphones on. As the music played, his enthusiasm for a song would find his hands drumming the rhythm on his legs.

'Now that's a tune, Ma,' he'd exclaim, having blasted the volume on the car radio. I enjoyed music of all genres and he liked to educate me on the latest. He and some of the crew had taken to learning Ed Sheeran songs – very wordy pieces with barely time for a breath. They would perform them in front of my TV before leaving the room with an air of electricity, generated by their intensity, still hanging in the air.

My mind leaps and I see him now down by the river, body rigid, eyes empty, looking blankly ahead. I hear myself scream. Inside I'm ripped apart in an instant, to the core of my being. I wonder where he got the cord I see around his neck. It's so cold and he's been out there all night. There's a bite in the morning air. It's still sharp as my lungs inhale. He has his winter jacket on – the one he loved, the one his dad bought for him, the one I was constantly grateful for as it was well insulated and a good defence against the cold wet weather. He feels cold. I try to hug him, to hold him, to feel him breathing. I know it's not possible but I'm willing it to happen anyway.

Two Gardaí are there, his dad and ... oh my God, I have to ring his sister! How can I tell her what's unfolded in front of me? His older sister, Ciara, in her second year in college, was staying over in her boyfriend's family home for the weekend. She is unwell with a fever and throat infection. I feel a lurch in my stomach as I dial her number and ask her to come as quickly as she can. I try to hold back the devastation in my voice, but she knows the gravity in my tone and responds in a gasp as her voice trails away and she hangs up.

I see his friends standing, shocked to the core at the scene they came upon minutes before his dad and me. It looks as if the air has been physically punched out of their bodies – the ashen faces, the uncharacteristic silence as they stand and stare blankly ahead. I can hear and see but I'm suspended in disbelief. Is this what they are feeling too? They are too young to be experiencing this for the second time amongst their peers. Not six months ago they buried their fourteen-year-old friend who left this world also by his own hand. Has my son followed him?

These three lads, who helped us look for him, didn't expect this outcome, nor did the others who roamed and checked the usual hideouts and hangouts they frequented. We had been out – his crew, me and the Gardaí – not weeks before, looking for another teen who eventually showed up cold and embarrassed by the attention she captured.

I'm drawn to the river as it runs alongside the scene and the chaos that's erupting as word spreads and the crowd gathers. The flow is constant, without interruption, without need to alter its course, even in the wake of its banks holding a horror show. I'm slammed back to reality as Ciara arrives screaming to see him, as the Garda tries to hold her back.

'Let her see him,' I scream. 'She needs to see him.' I follow her to his side. Her father, having completed the task of untying his son and laying him on the ground, grasps hold of his daughter to support her in this moment of horror. She kneels by her young brother and strokes his face and coat much like I did. She tries to hold him and hug him, but his eyes, wide and staring colder than the December air, never blink in recognition of any of us. She stares at his eyes and exclaims, 'He's not there anymore. He's gone. I needed to see that or I'd never have believed it.'

My mind can't understand the evidence I see before me. This cannot be real. That cannot be him, there must be a mistake. He is frozen in time, my child, my son. The sounds that escape my mouth come from a place I didn't know existed in me. I hear something similar from his sister. His father is subdued into a stunned silence. Each of us is trying to process a scene that has no resemblance to our lives to date. Time stops. It bears no meaning. Somehow I reach into myself and begin to call my family, our nearest and dearest, who recoil in despair as each respond to the devastating news with a resounding, 'NO!' A shroud of disbelief overwhelms each one and I'm struck once again by the water, relentless in its flow, oblivious to the pain and the tragic circumstance on its banks.

And then it's back to the house without him. I feel so empty. I want to be with him. A doctor materialises offering injections of Valium. I decline and Ciara accepts. My ex-husband, Dave, is gone to tell his partner and face the dilemma of whether or what to tell their three-year-old son.

The word is out. The network has been alerted and people begin making their way to our little house in our street in the small town where we live. For the second time in six months, the town is shaken to the core by this type of breaking news. I wrestle with the pain, the disbelief, the need to call my sister Louise, just landed in Australia on honeymoon. I take myself to the quiet of the bedroom where he usually lay and dial her number. Once again I have to say the words out loud – 'Our beloved Darragh is gone.'

Again the shock waves are audible across the miles as she struggles to comprehend. He, who dug the garden and helped decorate the marquee for their ceremony; he, looking so handsome at their civil partnership only months before; he, who was at their send-off dinner only a week before? He cannot be gone, surely? She and her new wife, Lisa, have to make the long journey home. I assure her we will wait for them.

The house fills. People arrive, incredulous, shocked and sympathetic – neighbours, friends, family and colleagues – most unable to find words. Some are carrying big pots of warm soup, stews and plates of sandwiches covered in foil. A friend offers to take away and finish the laundry, still in the kitchen where I had left it. I am deeply grateful.

We find ourselves – his father, sister and I – in this strange mist of disbelief, irrevocably changed by the events of the hours before. Each one of us in our own chamber of horrors as we grasp at fragments of information, piecing together his last hours as best we can. A photo taken that day on a phone as he helped decorate the community centre for the Santa's grotto is scrutinised for signs of impending devastation. He stares back at me from his mate's phone unmoved by my desperation to know something. And so begin the days of the rest of my now-altered life.

Chapter 2
No priest presiding

~

He sleeps silently amidst the sea of people, unmoved by the intensity of emotion or the wailing of the teenage girls. His 'crew' — the red-eyed, red-faced teenage lads — stand tall, arms linked, strong and stoic yet crumbling on the inside as they reflect on his antics, his quirky habits that made him unique and on the reasons they loved him.

The house is heaving with mourners, pale faced with shock, and with movers and organisers arriving with food in pots and on platters. All the while, he remains so uncharacteristically still. He is waxy in appearance. I sit by him and talk to him quietly. I ask him what he can see, feel and hear. How does it feel for him? I wait in anticipation for a flicker of movement, a response, a crack of a smile, noting at the same time my own ridiculousness. I stroke his hair. So short. I wish it was longer so I could feel more of it.

We didn't argue about those kinds of things and I'm relieved that we got on well for the most part. I smooth his shirt, feeling the strange padding that seems to be underneath. I wonder how they dressed him. I allow myself to dissolve into waves of tears, flooding me, submerging me. Somehow I keep breathing. Somehow I can receive the next person's condolences. Somehow I manage to open my mouth and words come out. I ask questions of the crew. We share funny memories and I feel the incredulity, the disbelief, theirs and mine, that this could be unfolding as it is.

The sandwich tray is waved in front of me again. I can see the triangles of neatly arranged bread with meat and salad sitting without ceremony on a plate I don't recognise. Egg mayonnaise and lettuce! How can such banality co-exist in the space where he is now laid out? 'You must eat!' I hear repeatedly, as yet another cup of hot tea finds its way into my hands.

So many stories from his fifteen years, recounted over days — everyone remembering their own special experiences with him, the last encounter now bearing such weight. Even mine now has to be the most forensically examined interaction I ever had with him. I listen to the account of the party the night before, where he danced all evening; the decorating of the youth club; the balloon he drew a face on and called his baby; the photo he posed for with the balloon and his mate which prompted the youth leader to cajole them into getting back to the task in hand. Just that day! That same Saturday! The usual boisterous energy of his crew replaced now with an eerie, stunned, disbelief. 'He was in great form,' I hear over and over.

So it wasn't just me who missed the signs then. I can already feel the strengthened bond this has created between me and his friends, as we are all catapulted into this new place. We spend time in his bedroom, too many people in the small space already altered by the messages penned on the whiteboard above his desk. These larger than life personas, usually spilling over with vitality, all cram into his room and tell a snippet of a memory that connects them to him. Some of the girls have already departed with soft toys and small keepsakes. His T-shirts become prized possessions. His joined-at-the-hip, best friend, usually boisterous, enthusiastic and prone to accidentally breaking things in his vicinity, is now speaking with a cracked voice as he wonders out loud, 'How could this have happened? Not him. Not Darragh. I wouldn't have expected this from him.'

Night falls and the crowds dissipate. I'm left with immediate family — Ciara, Dave, my parents and siblings — and a few close friends. The funeral has to be planned with extra thought, in light of our decision not to bring him up as a Catholic. This decision was first made after the birth of his sister, when the belief that a miracle such as a baby could be tainted with a sin on their soul and be anything less than perfect just didn't sit right with me or their father. That, coupled with the discovery, around the same time, of a book called *Conversations with God* prompted us to explore other avenues for our children's spiritual and moral development. However, at no time did we expect to be planning a funeral for our son, in a small rural town, without a blueprint in place.

Here we sit, this eclectic mix of people draped over arms of chairs and couches, crowded into one space. Ciara is shocked to the core; whiter than white, the youthful glow of her face is replaced with a pale, distant stillness as she twirls and twists a scrunched up tissue in her hands. Dave, broken into pieces; it is written all over his large frame. Slackened and almost crumbled, he tries to control his demeanour in the house he never shared with us. My parents, the grandparents, sit quietly inwardly wrestling with this awful truth that smacks them in the face. Their age lends no wisdom to make sense of this fate. My siblings Gregg, Ken and Louise, some of Dave's family and my long-time friends from my inner circle – each tense in the sustained disbelief that is still so prevalent in the room as we talk across his body, laid out between us, in that box we picked only hours before.

Dave and I, barely able to speak through the pain as we sat in the local undertaker's office, his living room, in fact; where happy, smiling family portraits lined the walls. I could hardly look in their direction. Quietly, the gentle voice of the very nice man whom I had occasionally passed in the street talked us through the details, the announcement in the paper that would need the decision as to where the service was to take place. His surprise that the local church would not be involved was too obvious to hide – a first for him, he announced, in thirty years as an undertaker. He needed to contact the gravedigger, and there were other jobs that he would undertake to do. The irony of the word struck me then – so that was why they were called 'undertakers'.

Shock still dominating, I sat tensely on the edge of his armchair, trying to absorb the details of the conversation – the informal setting for a very formal meeting. He beckoned us to follow him. I stood up on wobbly legs and willed them to walk out to the yard, out to the shed, to the line of boxes, some adorned in ornate gold and silver edges, not our likely choice. All lined up, stacked in rows, waiting to be filled with some human remains of a life that no longer existed. I wondered at the strange scene I found myself in. Dave and I nodded in agreement as we stopped at a plain model. Not too shiny, this long box would house our son's body. It was almost too much to absorb. And so it was done and the gentle voice spoke about invoices and costs and it somehow drifted over my head. How would this be paid for? The lack of spare funds in my accounts floated into my conscious mind and left again as quickly. Right then, it was about surviving the next few minutes without falling down. Back in our sitting room, one of my closest friends is holding a notepad and pen – Helen, the self-appointed chairperson we so desperately need to co-ordinate ideas. A stoic rock of support, the job of organiser imposed on her since college days, a role that comes so naturally to her. Ideas and suggestions spill out into the room over his body, laid out amongst us. Another of my friends has come armed with a poem called 'On Death of a Beloved', by John O Donohue, an acclaimed Irish author and poet whose connection to nature is profoundly healing. She passes the piece to me and as I read the opening line we all sit in reverence as the words give me strength and we know this will be included.

The note-taker, Helen, claims a piece from *The Prophet* as her contribution. In a strained voice, she reads, 'Your children are not your children. They are the sons and daughters of Life's longing for itself. They come through you but not from you, and though they are with you yet they do not belong to you.'

Encouraging children to foster their own truth of who they are is the message of this piece; they are arrows and we are the bows from which they are sent forth. It feels like a fitting sentiment to have present. We suggest songs and people volunteer to recount an event from his life or to read or sing. A notebook filled with outpourings of love and grief from the teenagers is brought down from his bedroom. My youngest brother, Ken, offers to take it home and choose an array of comments, keeping them anonymous, just in case it feels too much for the teen author on the day to have their name and comment highlighted. By the time everything is mostly decided, and the list of activities is read back to clarify, we are all bleary-eyed. It strikes me that Paula, one of my inner circle, will have a very long drive on this black, frosty night back to Wicklow. How can I entertain that additional concern with the enormity of what I am facing? Worlds meld, the everyday with the extraordinary. I can hear and see myself. I'm not split but I'm dually operating somehow, from some deep place, an automated place.

Thankfully, decisions are easily made, apart from an occasional tense moment as helpful suggestions cause a ripple of uncertainty. A venue is picked – the community centre where he spent his last day helping to decorate for Christmas feels like the most fitting.

People are incredible. A sound system from a local guy is offered and set up. Candles, helpers and logistics are all magically sorted. A ripped pair of trousers as a helper bends over to place a candle causes a stir of laughter, a welcome unprecedented tension breaker. The youth club leaders, offering their own response to the young people in the community, are ever-present offering help, taking care of logistics, things our little family cannot even conceive of. Friends rally around taking initiative and organising.

The community is strong and supporting our unusual request of no church; no priest is presiding. This small community is falling over themselves to make the ritual of the ceremony easier, to soften the blow to us any way they can. I'm so grateful. I hardly know some of the people who are offering their time, energy and skills to make this happen. Now each knows me as the mother of this child, this suicide victim.

The morning dawns. Dave spent the night by his side keeping guard. We swap shifts in the early hours. His dad leaves and I lay my exhausted mind and body on the couch beside him, my hand draped over the side of the coffin. I start to tell him to be with the light and to stay by us from where he is. I ask him to make sure he looks out for us; the little messed up family that loves him so. I'm so grateful for this time on our own – he and I, chatting, except his answers are inaudible.

I drift off into a very deep sleep, feeling cocooned for what was to be only twenty minutes. Time seems to be playing tricks and before long, the house is a swirl of activity again. I know he helped me in that quiet time so my body and mind can endure the day. Revived in spirit, I enter this fateful day, the day we really have to let his body leave our lives.

What to wear on this cold crisp day? Do I have a black coat? I'm surprised at the ordinary things that run through my head. Does Ciara have appropriate attire? She chooses a dress she wore to her paternal granddad's funeral some two years before. Some helpful friend has been through my stuff, and a coat has materialised on my bed.

Time ticks by. We have to close the coffin. The lid, closing on my beautiful son! Closing on my life as I have known it until now! The coffin filled with tears and love, with letters and trinkets from his friends, his portable speaker bringing music with him everywhere he goes. Ciara and I, holding on to each other, for life! I'm resolved. I feel stoic. There's no other option. A last-minute arrival from England barely gets to say goodbye. I witness again the shock and horror that cross his face as he sees such a young life now motionless, breathless; a child he knew since birth. I've been seeing that despair, that incredulous look for days now on men, women and young people. No words work. I wonder what's written on my face as I meet others.

His sister and I have our moment. My siblings and I have our goodbye. My sister Louise has returned hastily from her honeymoon in Australia, to have this inconceivable moment of goodbye with her nephew. Her immediate first response is of anger and frustration. 'What were you thinking?' she exclaims to which he gives no tinge of reply. If only he would sit up and say, 'I'm OK, I'm still here. It's all been a big mistake.'

Dave, his partner Sinead and his brothers and sister take their turn to have that last word, that last touch. Darragh's grandparents stand, digesting the scene, trying to come to terms with their young grandson laid out before them as they watch their own four children grapple with this strange and awful circumstance. And all the while, I'm there watching, in some observer mode, aware but feeling surreal.

The clamber in the hallway for coats and scarves, for tissues and strength! The house left bereft as the whole cacophony moves outside. Before long we are moving in procession, the road lined with people. I walk along barely aware of the sea of faces, an occasional start as I see an old acquaintance from another era. People from all aspects of my life and his are here in this small town to be at the funeral to support us. The green jerseys forming a line of honour; the team he ran on the pitch with week after week.

The waft of song on the wind as we near the community centre touches my heart. My new sister-in-law's beautiful voice caresses my brokenness as we make our way through the packed courtyard into the community centre. Only months before, looking so smart and standing so tall behind the pulpit, Darragh did a reading at her marriage to Ken. I'm awestruck, a candlelit pathway lines the entrance. It feels womb-like and nurturing as the little flames dance and flicker, creating an atmosphere of warmth and love. It gives me strength. We proceed and Dave begins and welcomes everyone. We read the chosen poetry. Louise's voice is strong yet broken as she reads, 'His Journey's just begun, don't think of him as gone away…' We share moments, listen, weep silently and sing.

I crack open even more when his crew begin their contribution with two of them singing 'Hallelujah', followed by another singing a song penned by one of them called 'Summertime'. They asked not to be seen as they struggle with emotion and their voices and music wash over us from backstage, behind the stage curtain. Three of my students sing a beautiful rendition of 'Stand by Me'.

This couldn't be more personal. The barber he loved to go to sings 'Bright Eyes', the most fitting description of him with those deep blue sparkling eyes. There's not a dry eye in the place. His uncle, Ken, reads the comments from the copybooks his friends have filled. We laugh as the truth of our burned shed is exposed and the perpetrator, his 'joined-at-the hip' friend, stands and takes a bow knowing his act was that of an accidental nature and his identity was held as secret in a loyal and trusted way by his best friend. Gregg, another uncle, tells the story of when Darragh, as a young child, carelessly spilt the holy water collected at the well on the Hill of Tara. Subsequently, Gregg had to rescue him as he fell in or was pushed by the disgruntled spirits as he tried to refill his bottle. His own baptism perhaps!

Poignant, beautiful, personal — we somehow created a ceremony to send him off. No one here knows what to expect, this is such a deviation from the normal activities of the community hall. This ritual, a ceremony designed by a family in the eye of a storm, honours his short life and sends him on his way. Each one wondering what had happened to the vibrant youth he presented before all who crossed his path. 'Darragh would talk to everyone' is a constant comment, not shy or retiring, his interest in people caused him to engage in conversation with all ages.

And then it's done. As the last song fills the cocooned space and spreads out across the silent yard, the coffin is wheeled to the door and loaded into the back of the funeral car. I'm cold to the core. I'm not sure if my legs will carry me. When I reach the door I become overwhelmed by the scene that meets me. The whole yard is overflowing with people braced against the cold wind.

I'm hoping it remained dry for the length of our ceremony. No one looks wet. Most stand reverently as we pass, some smile through tears and others remain rigid in their posture. Linked by my brother Gregg and Ciara, we follow on foot up through the town, each shop and doorway is lined with people. I can hardly take it in. Murmurs of conversation float alongside us in a quiet tone bearing a sense of respect. Children run up along the edge of the misshapen line, curious to see how it all looks from the front. I make some light conversation with no relevance, but the walk seems so long and arduous. I wonder how my elderly aunts are faring, hoping they drove behind. For the second time that day, I walk along slowly behind a car carrying him, now smothered with flowers.

A few words are spoken by Gregg, 'Let him fly free now knowing he filled his fifteen years to the brim with life and joy and mischief. May his life touch us with his magic for many years to come.' As he continues, the coffin is lowered; single roses, not fully open yet, are dropped in by those with a special bond to him. It has become a bit like a film now as it plays out in front of me. As I drop my flower down into the freshly dug hole that holds the box with my beautiful son's body inside, I wish it was a sunflower. He, Ciara and I planted seeds when they were younger. His fascination as they grew tall only dimmed in exasperation when one morning we awoke to find their stems had been broken. Young and full of questions, he couldn't fathom how anyone could ever interfere with such magic and so it became a tradition for us to plant these seeds every summer.

His love of nature couldn't be undone. Even in the midst of raging hormones he would come in to alert me to a beautiful moon on an evening. It's almost fitting that he chose to leave us in a place of nature, the grove of trees by the river's edge.

The graveside procession is long and I find myself standing alone. How cruel it is that there's nobody by my side I think, perhaps reflecting the depth of isolation felt by a mother in such a circumstance, and yet I know I'm deeply supported by many. I stand and hug with love every person that comes, struggling with their own grief, their own torment and disbelief as they meet me in mine. Feelings peak as I hug his after-school minder. He loved her and she him. Incredulity washes over me again. I can't believe what's happened. I see his primary school teacher of his last few years, the one he didn't get on with and his pre-school teacher whom he loved. This pattern has been repeated over the last few days so many times as particular people trigger memories and times in my life and his, now no longer possible to re-create because he's gone.

The long, long, line of young people becomes all that's left as they come to greet and hug me. I'm feeling transported into another frame. I'm supporting them and they me as we meet. There are hundreds of them — some familiar, more not. I have no awareness of anyone else around. Surely they haven't all gone and left me? It feels like I'm in a time–space vacuum, me and these teenagers filing in an orderly line, some in school uniform, some in civvies.

His crew had asked me to tell the principal they wished to dress in non-uniform. I cannot believe this would pose an issue. Who would care what they wear? They wear suits to honour him, because they know that even for a tracksuit-hoody guy he loved to get dressed up. Two family weddings in the past summer had given him opportunity to do just that. Ironically he is put to rest in his finery.

The rain comes and signals an end to this particular part of the day. A lift is offered and I gratefully accept. Most have left and the graveyard looks bleak and desolate with the rain save for a burst of colour where he has disturbed the landscape. Back in the local pub, I overhear some of the lads say they recorded the next song in our bathroom. I smile through the tears as the guitar starts and I remember the noisy band practices that filled my home, my garden, my life and occasionally my bathroom. Apparently the acoustics are better in there!

Surrounded again – by people, kind words, no words, hand squeezes, hugs, tears and connected embraces where only love speaks through feeling. The strange hugs I can't tolerate; the ones that feel patronising. Hands I have to remove from me, the life-sucking feeling, the ones that make me feel like I want to lie down and die. I'm noticing this heightened sensitivity. I'm selective in where I spend time, it's crucial, I'm trying to survive. I'm led by this deep interior part of me; it's an inside job, tactfully bringing me to places where I get comfort, nurturing and support. It's hanging in the balance. My son has died, he is fifteen … this can't be right, he did this to himself. Get your hands off me unless you are true in your feeling. I can't let you touch me. What is this awareness I'm feeling? My instincts are leading me, my words are limited and real and only the truth is spoken and heard.

Sometime later I find myself back at home, the return journey a blur. In the corner of my hallway, I feel immersed in a vortex of light as I stand embracing a friend and healer. He and I become one and I am enveloped in light. I wonder if anyone can see this as it comes to an end. Was that a split second or ten minutes? Later that night, as I try to sleep, the intense crying turns to laughter and the deepest love I've felt as my recent lover and long-time best friend, Derek, embraces me and exclaims: 'It's him! I can feel him and it's exquisite. It's beyond beautiful, he wants to show you.' I trust this man implicitly. I can get a sense of what he describes. We laugh and cry all at once. It's extraordinary. It's crazy. It feels so real. It's like an expanse of light and feeling, of love overwhelming my every cell. I'm out of control as is he, but it's beautiful. That's him. It has to be.

Chapter 3
Shine bright like a diamond

~

'Shine bright like a diamond' – the words of Rihanna pound over and over in my head. I'm down by the river at the tree where he departed. I'm with my sister, his sister and my brother – all of us living in a suspension of reality. It's barely a week since the funeral.

I've buried a crystal in the earth, asking that the land be healed and that no other young person leaves in this way from here. I'm following some inner message and it feels like something useful to do. The place is like a shrine. Tea lights everywhere, still flickering somehow despite the drizzle and the wind's efforts to quench them. His friends have left love notes and messages pinned on to the tree bark, teddies, packets of roll-up tobacco and bottles of yogurt milk, his favourite. I sit and breathe through the tears as the clouds part and a ray of sunlight hits the little scene under the trees.

I hear the words again, 'Shine bright like a diamond'. I feel like it's him trying to tell me something. Shine! I wonder. I'm barely holding myself up these days. Someone is always by my side as I go around shattered on the inside into many fragments, walking as my legs move in front of me but unsteady in my frame. It is far from shining I feel, yet I find solace in the words and music only I can hear. Meanwhile, the river runs by undeterred by our little party; this sad, disconsolate party of five. The tree, forever altered, as his dad sawed the branch – the offending piece of wood that provided the ledge from which he could … I shudder to continue that thought.

I watch as a procession comes towards us, a sea of blue jumpers, as the school pauses for a break and the once inconspicuous grove of trees has become a pilgrimage for the teenagers. Most of his crew haven't made it back to a structured day in school yet. The procession comes to a pause when they see us and silence descends over the entourage. I address the group, reminding them there's nothing any of them could have done in this instance. It's not their fault. I cannot continue. My brother Gregg pleads with them from some fundamental deep place: 'Please talk to each other. Support each other. Lean on one another. Let him be the last.' There's a deep sense of solemnity as Gregg speaks from the core of his being; his choked words carry a strength that I know in every part of me those young people heard if not with their ears then with their souls. This sense of knowingness is like a flame within me that ignited sometime immediately after his parting. Time is so immaterial now; days of the week, times of the day, none of it matters.

Our piece said, I want to leave his friends to have their time in this newly enshrined piece of ground. We drive to a café to get some lunch. I wonder if I can even eat when I hear Rihanna singing 'Shine bright like a diamond' over the café's speakers. Coincidence or him, I ponder. I watch people having lunch, engaged in conversation, meaningful perhaps to them. Two little pig-tailed girls, each quietly fingering a bun as their mum buys a few minutes' silence reading the newspaper. They are munching away, faces decorated by chocolate smudges. I feel separate from all of life in the bustling café, sitting with my shattered heart trying to do normal things like eat, be, converse or find a point to any of it.

Over time, the song becomes like an anthem for me. It turns up in my head, in the car, in the shop, always making me pause, helping me to feel through my pain and tears, feel the light that I am, that he was. A deep sense of connection to all, there is no separation. 'Yeah, yeah, yeah,' my mind usually kicks in. 'Try living this life, try waking up every morning to this reality. Why, oh why, did he choose this? What was he thinking? What did I not do? What could I have done? This is the most painful of separations. Who am I talking to? God?'

Divine Spirit is my preferred choice of reference for the Greater

Intelligence of the Universe. From my new perspective, Greater Intelligence isn't the first thing that comes to mind, more like 'pointless waste of potential, life and possibility'. All of my core values are shaken to the roots now. My beliefs crumble like clay shaken from a pulled garden flower. I was that flower, blossoming as a believer in the innate goodness of all people, even families in the direst of circumstances that I came across in social care. I trained under many inspirational teachers in the ways of the life force and energy medicine. They brought me, as a young explorer, to so many wonderful insights and to awareness. For years I worked with energy, that unseen force that surrounds us all, helping people find balance and their own inner guidance. The privilege of sitting opposite someone, being totally present to them, holding space and allowing healing to unfold, is one I constantly lived in appreciation of.

Over time, I experienced a deep connected love for people I hardly knew as I watched them gain awareness or unveil a truth to themselves. I participated regularly in groups and felt connected to a greater love than a human's experience. Only a week before Darragh's suicide, I found myself enveloped in a bubble of love for all humanity as I sat in a large circle of people gathered together to invoke healing and light into our lives under the guidance of one such inspirational teacher. Little did I know what was coming! I am totally frustrated at the thought. Somewhere in me a belief had fostered that living in this way would be a safeguard against such awfulness; apparently not in this case.

I wondered now how pointless the exercise appeared to be. He had love, he was loved and he knew that he was loved. He had homeopathy, energy medicine, all of his life and this was the outcome? This craziness? This end? His choice mocked me. It made my choices need scrutinising. What if I had ...? The rest of this sentence runs over and over again, bringing me into a spiral of unanswered questions; a totality of possibilities, too many to conceive. And then I look at his sister: stoic, strong, resilient and independent. How can that be? She came through the same life with the same parents, the same choices made for her. Now she is making her own decisions, the most recent being not to stay at home since his passing. 'It is just too painful to sleep here anymore,' she says. I get it but this adds to the incessant need to ask myself what has happened to my life? The way out of this spiral of questions, which is driving me out of my mind, is by actively commanding that it stops, just for now, just for a moment's reprieve.

It's a Saturday morning a couple of weeks after the funeral. I awake and feel the need to get out of the house, as the walls are closing in. I go for breakfast in a nearby local town. It's such early days and I feel very sorry for my lot. As I turn my car in the car park, an elderly woman with a crutch beckons me. It transpires she needs a lift as, true to Irish weather, there is a shower pending. She's only in the car a few moments when she tells me that she picks up my sadness and explains to me she is a fortune teller and that himself wants me to know he is really happy. She continues to astound me with details of how he left the world, describing his character, telling me he has only one sister and that she will be OK. She will let him go in her own way and in her own time. This is an important comfort to me, as I wonder how the impact of his act will inform her life from here on in.

The woman has my full attention and to top it all she asks for €150 for the impromptu reading. I have very little cash on me and she suggests we drive to a bank machine, which I naively do. I give her only a third of her fee as it's as much as my account will allow. Although I know she is taking advantage of my vulnerability, her information is so accurate and our meeting is so random, I hardly know what to do in the situation. I never set eyes on her before or since that day. I drive the short distance home, astounded at the audacity of the woman asking me to pay her for the lift I gave her and equally incredulous at the haphazard way I encountered her and the evidence of life after death she presented to me.

A few nights later, I'm sitting up in bed journaling, as sleep escapes me. Journaling has helped me from a young age to process my emotions as I purge all the feelings uncensored out onto a page. This particular evening I finish with a plea to Darragh to give me something to keep me going, some piece of evidence. Yes, I am insatiable in this and nothing save his physical presence will satisfy me. I am like an addict looking for the next fix, the next piece of evidence that he still exists somewhere out there. I slump eventually into a sleep and am rudely awakened by a pillow on my head. I am totally thrown into panic as my mind tries to assess the situation. Adrenalin floods my already stressed body and then I begin to laugh out loud. I am home alone. I had placed the pillow behind me before I began writing and obviously it fell on me as I slid down the bed in slumber. But is it just a precariously placed pillow or his intervention? I like to think he was nudging me into some lightness in the face of my raw feelings and despite the adrenalin rush, sleep returns easily.

Chapter 4
Music and song

The deafening quiet poses such a stark contrast to the raucous laughter and echoes of the young teenage men as they file in the door. Testosterone-fuelled, singing, dancing, competing, performing, they bring his absence to me more painfully than I could have imagined. Yet, I am so grateful for their visits: the incessant dialogue, the constant demanding and interrupting of one another, their song practice, the in and out of the front door and all the while, my tears of joy and laughter are etched with pain too. The witty guitar player begins an intro and after a bout of nervous laughter, they sing the poignantly worded song that they practised for me in harmonies. 'Timshel' by Mumford and Sons – a song that we all knew he loved and was played at his funeral service.

And death is at your doorstep
And it will steal your innocence,
But it will not steal your substance,
And you are not alone in this
You are not alone in this,
As brothers we will stand
And we'll hold your hand, hold your hand.
You are the mother,
The mother of the baby child
The one to whom you gave life
And you have your choices

These are what made man great,
His ladder to the stars.

As I listen with tears cascading silently down my face, I am astounded by the sensitivity of these young men in what appear to be oversized bodies. 'We are in this together, we thought that was pretty apt,' they say when the song ends and I try to gain composure. His joined-at-the hip friend, who stopped in most evenings to our house to play the Xbox, is a bit reluctant in his singing debut. He visibly struggles with the absence of his mate in these familiar surroundings. Another, the nifty footballer who is small in stature and could eat for Ireland, is often teased about the quantity of food he consumes in one sitting. He is fast catching up on the others in size.

Despite the recent habit of smoking that some partake in, these lads are fit and fast on the GAA pitch. Their constant banter, jokes and witty jibes at each other evidently mask potent sensitivity and connection. It is truly a moment of love we share in these unprecedented and unusual circumstances. But here, now, we are in exceptional times as we each try and adjust to his loss. They are used to my tears, they see this often on a visit, but tonight there's a special magic. It's the summer and it's another season beginning, another segment of time marked since his departure now six months ago.

I ache inside for his voice, his gangly frame, his input and his mortification at the lads feeling so free in front of his ma. I wish him to be here in the midst of the madness that transforms my living room and transports me back to a time half a year ago when such things were commonplace. The next piece of performance is more vigorous. The song is set up on someone's phone and is connected to the base speaker. As the lull of the slow beat starts, they pretend to be chilled out and relaxed. Suddenly, with a start and right on cue, at the exact moment the pace of the music quickens, they all jump up and dance like crazy in a circle. One of them drops a torch out of his pocket and it lands, switched on, right in the middle of the melee. I know instantaneously that's his way of partaking – this is Darragh in the middle of the madness having a moment with the crew. 'Nice of

Darragh to join us,' one of them quips when he sees the torch spinning at his feet.

Sitting in the silence after they bustle out the door, I recall my dream of the night before where I was with him and his crew in a bar and a dance-off began. He was in the middle of it, loving it, and I said to him, 'Stay, stay, look at the fun you're having,' to which he replied, 'It's too late, Ma, I've already left.' How apt that seems now as the loud silence impregnates the space. I look at his smiling face framed forever behind the glass, hoping for a glint in his eye, a twinkle of life, a spark of reason. Nothing happens. Eventually I blow out the candles and ascend the stairs to the empty room. I glance in at his bed. I cannot resist the need to lie there, to stare up at the 'stars' he created by blowing bits of scrunched up paper out of the end of his pen. 'Spit wads' they call those. I shudder at the idea and wonder what was in his mind as he lay there.

How many times did he ponder over this thing that he did? Were there months of planning? Did he decide that day? What really precipitated this? Was it the unsettledness in school? We had even discussed the possibility of leaving school and pursuing other options like an apprenticeship. Intelligence wasn't the issue. His lack of understanding for the need for such stifling boundaries and boredom resulted in his bad habit of distracting himself and others in class. I know this line of thinking brings with it so many unanswered questions and so, with reluctance and weariness, I stand up and leave his room before I undo the good the evening's events had generated.

As I lie in my own bed, I marvel at how the whole evening's scenario unfolded – my chance meeting with the guitar-playing, singer-songwriter of his crew earlier; my desire to tell him what the medium had said: 'Stay with your music, don't give up on your dream.' Music, drumming in particular, was a big interest to Darragh, my member of the crew. This mix of young ambition, raw talent and various musical abilities entertained the neighbourhood when the band practised in our kitchen. There, Darragh's drum kit imposed on our aesthetics and broke the sound barriers. Eventually the drums were retired to the back garden shed, where they were fated to be burned into fragmented twisted shards of metal in an accidental fire.

I think now of the debacle of the shed burning, his panicked voice on the phone. 'Our sheds are burning. I called the fire brigade first,' Darragh says, sounding breathless. I am at the school, en route from work to collect Ciara and help transport her heavy book-filled bag. It's the Easter holidays and it's a wild windy day. I abandon my task instantly and arrive at home in minutes to be met by concerned neighbours out on the road and a few members of Darragh's crew sheepishly standing by. I meet Darragh who has singed hair and a pale shocked face. The sirens scream as they pull into the cul-de-sac and we are ushered out of the way. Ciara arrives laden with her backpack; her indignation fades to disbelief when the scene greets her. She drops the heavy bag and runs into the house. I follow her and we are immediately instructed by a fireman to leave as the house could be at risk. 'The oil tank has buckled,' he says. 'This could be extremely dangerous.'

I can barely fathom what's unfolding. Wild red flames lick the oil tank as one shed and then two are swept by the unrelenting fiery beast. All our tools, his drums and even the wall plaster were brought to ransom by this fireball. It's a challenge to bring this flaming wildness to an end but the firemen do their job and eventually a smelly smouldering wet pile of debris is all that is left of our back garden. Darragh stands with an arm around me and Ciara, protective of us, the man of the house. My mind begins to race into the why, the how and the who done it. That mystery took a while longer to unravel.

I toss and turn as this memory floods me. What a difficulty sleep posed that particular night as my mind considered all the awful outcomes of teenagers and burning buildings. Darragh would only say it was an accident and that although it was not him who started the fire, it was his fault, and added that no one was smoking in the shed. He was full of remorse as the enormity of the possible outcome impacted on him. Some of his crew came over the next day to help with the immediate aftermath. A week later, my friend Sharon organised, as a surprise for me, a clean-up party for people to come and help us with an all-hands-on-deck approach. That team, armed with wheelie bins, shovels and picks, did Trojan work, clearing sooty piles, cutting back and removing charred and burned plants. We enlisted Darragh and some of the possible perpetrators to help. They agreed willingly and we created some semblance of a garden in an afternoon.

Over the days of the funeral, his best mate disclosed that he had been playing with a lighter, burning tiny fragments of the carpet underlay so it melted into a lovely pattern: 'I lit it and watched the pattern form and then put it out. At least I thought it had gone out,' he said, somewhat subdued in his delivery. The flimsy underlay that was supposed to soundproof the walls cost Darragh his drum kit and me my shed and sense of safety.

The night passes into the early hours and I'm still awake thinking about what kind of mother I was. The recounting of the shed incident, now a funny story, brings up all these questions again. Was I working too much and not paying enough attention? Did I do enough? The earlier quest to stop this futile line of thinking is not so successful this time.

Funny, how spending time with the crew often has this effect as it highlights the paradox of remembering life, with the sometimes excessive exuberance of teenage hormones, and the painful stillness that fills the nothingness now. Many sleepless nights like this become the norm. I try meditation but my mind won't shut up; writing, but I'm too tired to make the pen work; reading, but my concentration is disastrous.

In a last ditch effort to get some rest or at least to stop the incessant wondering about my parenting, I recall my visit to a medium the previous week. Ciara, following a recommendation from a friend, had visited her first, and she had been an incredible support, gaining Ciara's confidence pretty quickly in the reading. A few nights prior to Ciara's visit, I had begged Darragh, yet again, for a sign. Burdened with the heavy load, I was in desperation. In my sleep he came and stood leaning over me singing, 'Don't you worry child, don't you worry child, see heaven has a plan for you'. He urged me to wake up and write down the words. In my exhaustion, I declined. However, I remembered the encounter the next morning.

I related the story to Ciara, each of us still hungry for any little fragment of story or connection with him. Early in Ciara's session, the medium describes Darragh as young, vibrant and singing as he arrives in to their communication. She reveals the words he is singing to her as those of my dream. Ciara is so enthralled by this that the medium now has her full attention. Information seems to be easily accessible to this woman about his life, their lives as siblings and their shared experiences. How could she have known about the night Ciara lay in bed devastated that her brother had gone and felt as if the blankets were being brought up around her neck, enveloping her with love? How could she know his quirky habit of coming to sit way too close to her on the couch as she watched her favourite soap opera and whispering, 'you need to get a life' before leaping up and disappearing out the front door? Whatever the beliefs one holds about this there was no doubting this woman knew things.

On the morning of my reading, due to a series of misadventures, I drive unaccompanied instead of with a friend. Travelling alone along the relatively new motorway to Carlow, fields and trees swish by in soft focus adding colour to the hour-long journey. Anticipation is humming through my cells as I wonder what I might experience. At the beginning of my session, it feels like a game of name guessing, as people I haven't even heard of seem to be coming to the medium. My confidence is waning, disappointment hovering and I wonder if what I had envisaged would unfold. But then, 'He's here,' she says, 'the one you came for'.

Relief and anxiety hit me all at once. He says I'm run down and I need to take better care of myself. I want to laugh at the irony. I'm carrying a lead weight crushing my being; of course I'm run down. She describes his eyes, his big brightly shining blue eyes, his wide cheeky smile, his sense of music and love of dance. She tells me he's dancing in the light now. 'He was too light for this world. He couldn't stay any longer,' she adds. I'm crying now, grasping the details, willing her to have more, to tell me more. I feel like an addict again desperate for a fix.

She says I connect with him regularly in my dreams. I know this especially of late. Much as she did with Ciara, that woman tells me things about my son, a teenager she never met – how fond of his hair gel and deodorant he was; how he loved sausage sandwiches and drank milk by the litre. Her insight is phenomenal.

I leave that medium's sitting room all mixed and stirred up, grateful for the empty car so I can try and process what has just happened. As the memory of that incredible interaction fills my mind I try and will myself to sleep, taunting myself with the possibility that maybe tonight, after all the singing and dancing of the crew in the house, Darragh will connect with me in my dreams. Eventually, I drift off.

Chapter 5
A worthy cause

~

Stormy sea thrashes rocks, momentous in its white spray. I sit and watch, seeing but not seeing, breathing through a heavy heart as the waves reflect my own turbulent waves, my emotions, thrashing my body. Another sleepless night filled with the relentless questions – what ifs; should haves, could haves and why didn't I? The unravelling of every decision I ever made, back to meeting, dating and marrying his dad. It's a tiresome pursuit that now commonly invades the small hours of the night.

This pattern of mind trying to make sense of the insane presentation of facts; feelings swirling like tidal pools waiting to break the surface: fear, sadness, despair. Why him? Why us? Why me? My space is empty, the now vacuum of a nest that was our home, as even his sister takes refuge elsewhere, as the pain is too deep for her to remain in that space.

Time passes with no acknowledgement here on the outcrop of rock, off the pier in Dún Laoghaire, until eventually the crisp cold air signals me to move. I gingerly take myself indoors into a café where I can sit anonymously. The din of conversation, the bang and clash of cutlery, the grinding legs of furniture as it moves to accommodate the next tea drinker. Life as it continues for those who know nothing of this place I inhabit. The distant melody, voices, laughter, I hear without hearing. The family that bustles their way in beside me, awkward body movements as they take turns to remove the outer layers of clothing, that protect against the chilly wind. Half nodding, half smiling as they impose on my space momentarily before settling in to quiet conversation, oblivious to the turmoil within me, the tired-faced, weary woman seated next to them. I'm reminded of a time when we were such a family out for the day, walking in the wild weather, tasting the spray of the seawater along the Irish coastline as we, my little family, enjoyed days in nature.

I tried to go to work today, unsuccessfully as it turned out. Some mornings I awake from a tearful, tiresome, broken sleep and pull myself out the door to my ever wonderfully supportive colleagues and staff. Always an unwritten understanding – if you cannot take class today I will cover for you. My classes are usually a welcome distraction and I need to stay present and in the moment as we discuss all manner of theories and experiences in many arenas of life. Me and a group of adult learners in a symbiotic relationship – an agreement whereby we show up in the best condition we can for the day's learning and sharing about everything from personal effectiveness to care of the elderly and parenthood.

Ironic that seems now. Darragh took that particular confidence from me. How can I stand as a voice on parenting when my particular style resulted in catastrophe? The ultimate failure as a parent! The stages of adolescence never completed in his case. His search for identity not realised. Today I cannot keep my end of the bargain; I cannot present myself as ready for work and available to those learners. And so the water called to me as it does sometimes. I feel the enormity of the body of water, the waves relentless in their pursuit of the shore, still visible from my window seat and I am reminded of the cycles of life, the continuum that is life and somehow my problems and I seem to shrink.

My phone summons my attention and I see it's Helen, one of my inner circle, the close group that have been watchful of me since this whole thing unfolded. Her voice immediately senses I'm in a raw and vulnerable place. I'm invited to her home for a *meeting about me* the following evening. It's about as much conversation as I can engage in for now as I need to maintain my composure in this public space, and so I agree to be available to attend the following evening and decline a lift. She covers all possibilities in offering support to get me there.

The following evening I arrive in curious interest to Helen's home, most of my drive spent pondering this unusual invitation. I'm greeted by an array of friends and siblings — this core group purposeful in their demeanour. I'm assured it is all in good intention for me. I'm somewhat disconcerted but I know and trust everyone in the room to a high degree. Teas and coffees in hand the meeting begins. They have been witnessing the struggle that has become my life experience. They feel helpless and wish to support me. A suggestion arises: if they could find a way to support me financially would I consider taking time off work and going away, taking time out from the structures and routines that currently both stress and support me. I am completely overwhelmed as I see the love and support that's been extended to me in the most sensitive way. Each person there is a very close friend or family member; each is willing to volunteer time and practical help in making this suggestion a reality.

I find myself reeling with a sense of anticipation, fear, and uncertainty. An agenda is set with a timetable and a list of jobs. Each person willingly volunteers to take on a piece of work. All I have to do is consider the proposal and decide where might serve as a healing place for me to go and for how long. Through the tear-stained windscreen I find it hard to focus on the drive home. I know I am blessed with the people I have around me. This is not news to me, but nonetheless there is something inordinately special about the events of this evening.

Sleep again escapes me until the early hours as my mind reels with possibility and fears. How could I just leave work in the middle of a year? What would Ciara think? In some deep part of me I know I will go for it. I knew on the way home that evening that I had no choice, but my mind continues to throw up as many protestations as it can.

Budgets and financial problems fill my over-active mind until eventually a haze of sleep spares me a few hours of working out possibilities. The mornings are quiet now. No longer our little family going through the motions each day, in the machine of life in the western world. Gone are the rows when he would resist getting up for school. My dilemma of needing to get out the door to work and wanting to make sure he was up and on his way frustrated me – the rushing around, the uniform debate, the lunch and dinner considerations, who eats what and what time we can sit down to dinner, the discussions about homework that hardly ever got done with any degree of care and attention, the debates over bedtime, Xbox, too many lads in the house, the remote control, time to be in, phone use, internet, loud music, too much deodorant ... The endless list of simple, ordinary, life concerns that most houses with teenagers expect and live through without much time for pause. A life mundane in these ordinary family issues that presented daily is so radically different now, changed literally overnight.

Now it's just me most of the week, in and out of a still, quiet, space where he smiles from two-dimensional spaces off walls and shelf spaces, captured in a moment in time. I sit in the evenings and look at him, yearning to hear his voice, remembering all manner of chats, fun, dance lessons and conversations. Often times, memories from when he was only a baby flood me with no warning or apology – so real, so relentless in their painful presentation, as if a reel of film unwinds into my mind, showing me that life I had as a mother and he as a baby and child.

By the second meeting about me in Helen's house I have picked an island in Thailand where a friend lives half the year. It sounds and looks idyllic and feels safe as I know that a friendly face will be in the same vicinity. The momentum grows as the group pools resources and ideas. A benefit night is coming together. I am struggling all the while with this reality. A benefit night unfolding for me! Were those things not for worthy causes? Was I that now? I feel almost embarrassed by the idea and yet this is out of my hands. My God, has my life got no point of control? I'm living on the edge of craziness. Pack up and go to Thailand without my lover, without my friends, without my son or daughter? What is going on? I'm living on the energy of my supportive friends and it's so well intentioned. Inside I'm feeling like I want to scream, 'STOP! All of you, stop! I love you, I love what you are doing, this is all fine and grand but I just want my old life back.'

And so I fall apart at the meeting. I express all that angst, the fears, the out-of-control feelings. I can do that. I have that level of communication with these people. They hear me. They tell me how it is for them — the helplessness they feel watching me wrestle with the vast torrent of emotions I feel. They tell me they wonder how I face into each day knowing that he is not here. They tell me I am living every parent's worst nightmare. They tell me they are crying out to do something, anything that may ease my pain even a little. We eat cake and drink tea and laugh a little as the plans continue to unfold. I can finish up work around Christmas, a natural break in the calendar, and take a month or two to get ready to go.

Time marches on and I tell my students I'm taking special leave. I'm overwhelmed by the raw honesty with which I speak and am received. For a moment in time professional boundaries are held in suspension as we meet in unchartered waters, human beings relating, living and feeling the raw truth of what it is to be human. I realise that the level of respect and integrity I receive is a tribute to how well I have been holding myself together. I have stayed real and true to myself and my emotions and yet could get out of my own way enough to stay present to those people at the same time. An understanding is evident. It's unsustainable under the conditions I'm living in. I walk away with head held high knowing that something new is unfolding.

Special leave is unpaid and renders me ineligible for social welfare support. Discussion with the banks to suspend mortgage payments leaves me an emotional wreck for days. The boxes that are ever so important to all institutions in our society once again stresses me to breaking point, when after three calls and a deliberation of every expense that I incur daily, I finally dissolve into a catastrophic mess. I don't belong in your boxes! My son killed himself! Can I just have a few months off so I can take time to recover? Why does this take three attempts with the same painful processes and lists of questions? 'My circumstances are changed but not since our last call. Yes, the direct debit bounced. I tried to set up a moratorium on this account. In fact, I was assured that was in place so why another call? And why did you go looking for money that was not there?'

And now I'm spluttering and crying all over the phone. I'm not sure I am making sense. Now the bank knows I'm a failure as a parent as well as trying to be a responsible mortgage payer. It's all too much. I hang up and feel like life is just not worth it. I wonder if I hadn't worried so much about paying bills might I have been home more with him and his sister. Instead I spent years with two part-time jobs, one with children in care and one in adult education, and when possible I worked with people in a direct healing capacity one evening a week. Very busy, very intense, using up the juice in my tank so my bills got paid. Did I neglect the real important stuff? It takes time to recover myself after this call.

How can our society be so dehumanised? With all the computers and technology the system failed to complete the process and my arrangement was left pending, so the process was incomplete and hence the extra stress. A human response might have gone off-script long enough to hear the strain in the voice, to realise this was a responsible person trying to make a plan for the payment to resume further down the line. How many people have been down this road, feeling so stressed because they owe money to a large financial institution, being met by an unfeeling script when human existence has so many variables that cannot be boxed neatly to fit? We live in a society whereby the assumption is that people are untrustworthy. Form filling is of paramount importance, checklists that justify the existence of a position in an organisation.

Cynical of me perhaps, but in my world none of that matters! In my world friends are organising an event so I can live away for six weeks without pressure. In my world, connection with people on a real level matters. Nature matters, love is paramount in its many expressions. People supporting each other in difficult times, in insightful and creative ways, is what matters. The paradox of my existence never ceases to amaze me. Love and pain in juxtaposition, equally poignant!

Some months pass and the event is happening. It's dusk on the night of the worthy cause concert. I've been in bed for most of the afternoon as wave upon wave of devastation flood me. The good-hearted people around me are, thankfully, oblivious to the level of despair I am feeling. 'Not now, not tonight,' I say to myself as my mind wrestles with the emotion, 'but, too many are counting on me being there'. The pressure feels enormous. It's ironic that sometimes goodwill and intent can feel like such pressure. There's a lot at stake here. I have signed up for and agreed to the big trip away and it all pivots on tonight's gig. I wonder how I will make it to the shower never mind to my partner's, where he will take over the rest of the drive. Somehow I drag myself to the bathroom and dress for an evening out. Puffy-faced and red-eyed, it looks like I've been in a boxing ring.

A fleeting moment of fear makes itself known as I wonder what if people don't actually arrive. The bleak February evening is hardly enticing to even the best intentioned. However, I remind myself that at least there will be the bus from the remote village of Moone where Mary-Pat, one of my inner circle, lives. The bands alone generated enough excitement for a bunch of people to have a knees-up and support the broken mother into the bargain. These bands draw a crowd of their own usually but this has been pitched as a benefit gig.

'Worthy Cause', 'Benefit Gig' – I still wrestle with this feeling. How can I just stop work and let people raise money for me to live on and not only that but head away on? The thought of not working and being around the house and this town every day is too painful to consider. But in truth, work was becoming too difficult to sustain. I feel smothered, confused and trapped by these feelings. Staying under the duvet for months on end would be the likely outcome. In fact getting back in there now is tempting.

'Get out of the house,' I shout to myself, 'and get going'. There have been enough under-the-duvet hours, more than most would know, one of the benefits of the now empty nest. Stopping at his photo on my way out the door I sternly rebuke him for causing such upheaval and torment. 'You have turned our worlds upside down with this madness,' I say, not for the first time, to his picture. I ask him also to support this evening's activities and especially to support me and his sister tonight. I am disappointed his crew cannot be part of the event, as this venue has a reputation for excellence but they are strictly prohibited from attending because it serves alcohol and they are under age.

The drive to my partner Derek's house is easier than I imagine. Thoughts of gratitude flood me. So many people got behind this whole idea. Tickets were printed by a guy my sister's beloved knows. Each of my inner circle, close family and beyond, organised, bought and sold tickets inbetween their own life's commitments and challenges. Gratitude is a welcome relief from the angst of earlier.

Arriving at Derek's, my fragility resurfaces. I let go a little of some of the tension as he embraces me and he drives the rest of the way. It's a week night in the city and drizzle makes my vision blurry, as do the watery tears that hover at the corners of my eyes. Again, I focus on gratitude for the well-intentioned supporters of my healing and this helps. As we near the venue I am relieved to see some familiar faces there already. I wait at the door for Ciara and her boyfriend to arrive. Then I lead the small group around to the side door to enter the music bar. I have no ticket. It is in the car that Derek has gone to park. I smile at the irony as I pay the €15 entrance fee in to my own fundraiser.

The first band playing tonight are three amazing musicians, singers and friends, called 'Savage Jim Breen'. They are fronted by a breath-of-fresh-air, life-affirming friend James who was my son's drum teacher. I could feel the resonance between James and himself immediately and used to wonder if Darragh would be like this guy in later years. Alas now, that will never be known. These will be followed by the ten-piece band 'Proudfoot', a rocking mix of brass and strings with a dynamic, charismatic lead singer and front man, Ger, a friend of old that came through my sister. He and his wife have three children of their own to look after; they reflected the level of goodness that exists in the world with their immediate offer to perform for no fee and somehow his other nine band members also agreed.

The early band gets up and running quickly and I am teary with gratitude as they play their hearts out to a swelling audience. So many show up! So many dance the night away, so many laugh and smile and embrace each other and me. As the night unfolds I'm catapulted into a polarity of feeling – I am a celebrity of sorts surviving great trauma, living the nightmare, trying to break out and do something different. It feels like my birthday, so many faces I know and love; people I worked with, from my various workplaces. A student from my early teaching days, now all grown up, triggers a whole new emotion of how life continues to evolve. I'm open inside, raw, broken and wounded. None of you know I spent half the day trying to drag myself out of an abyss of sadness to get here. Can you see that as I smile in pure gratefulness and love? The music fills the room and the dance floor is busy as the night unfolds. There is a tangible feeling in the room known for its music and song. A feeling of love!

The highest expression of what it is to be human. This is not just me! This is many, moved by the support, by the love, by the people in the room. We collectively made magic as the band gave it their absolute best and rocked the house and somehow I know he is there, in the midst of it, smiling at us all.

Chapter 6
Social welfare

I'm standing in line in the local social welfare office, a flood of emotions washing over me as I try to hold it together. My fellow line occupiers are a mix of foreign accents, impatient children jumping on chairs as parents try to rein them in and an occasional builder off a site. I'm struck by the lack of privacy in the space. The drab surroundings are furnished sparsely with a line of plastic, uncomfortable-looking chairs bolted to the floor in the middle of the room. Windows with partitions line the wall edges where one-on-one sessions happen. Everyone else stands in line for the larger opening at the end of the room.

The personal details of hatch window seven's life float into the space. I can hear every word. He became unemployed as work ran out on site, a story repeated window after window. Ordinary details carry a sense of urgency, the balance of power caught in the detail. I'm hanging on by a thread, clutching my pile of paperwork. They don't need to know my entire story I decide or I won't make it. I'm just working part-time and over the summer I'll need assistance. I'm entitled to it, everyone tells me. Inside I'm dying and wrestling with my beliefs. How can I be here in this line for the first time ever in my life, now after all I've been through? I worked so hard all my life, am I arrogant in my discomfort? A child's cry interrupts my thoughts and I'm nearly grateful as this distraction takes us all momentarily away from hatch window seven's details. Yes, he is married and no, his spouse is not working. As I listen without listening I sense the disempowerment of people as they bare their souls to over-worked, seemingly insensitive people who have, as yet, been unable to take a breather from the recession's tsunami of unemployed people. Ordinary wonderful people I'm sure, with problems, stresses, families and homes to deal with, but this feels really off.

As I inch forward to my assigned window, I'm gripping myself from the inside out in a tight structured fragility that's so precarious. As my ticked boxes are checked, I notice a barely perceptible softening of attitude towards me. I wonder why this is. Is it because I'm a tutor? A professional? Irish? My mind muses over anything to keep off the subject. Please don't clarify how many dependants I have. I'm nearly shifting in my seat trying to discreetly discuss the particular circumstances which have led me in here to this surreal experience.

Almost at the finish line and there's a stall: my employer classified my time in hours not days so it cannot be processed as is. How can such a small insignificant detail matter so much? I'm screaming inside now, the walls of the dam bursting. I can feel the waves of emotion flood me. I'll need an edited letter. 'But,' I exclaim, incredulously, 'it all adds up to the same time.' I'm trying to explain that, as it's an educational facility, it will be harder to contact personnel. The indifference sends me over the edge and I dissolve into floods of tears. I no longer care. I just need to get out of there. I'm grappling to end the interaction with some shred of poise but I'm way past that now. I almost run out of the space. I stumble out into the day's sunlight and try to gather myself. I'm embarrassed at the level of emotion and my loss of control in a public office. Completely disempowered, I feel like I'm begging for a little financial assistance with my heart gaping open. My body is shook to the core, incredulous that I can't pay my bills.

Well-meaning family and friends had been pushing me to seek financial assistance and I balked at the idea. I don't care if I'm entitled. I don't care about boxes on forms. I don't care how I ended up here or how many years I've paid taxes. I just want to live quietly, pay my bills and try and piece my life back together. Don't they realise my son is gone just like that? My child killed himself and they want me to fit into a box!

My life feels so surreal. I cannot fathom any of it. What is this charade we are calling life? How did I end up in this game? I don't like the game and I'm playing by rules that make no sense to me. Where's the humanity in our system? Why is there glass between me and the woman behind the desk? So many things race through my mind as I wait for the tidal wave to subside and for my body to try and regulate itself and get to breathing with some ease. I sit silently stunned after the sobbing stops and I try to focus. I watch so-called normality all around me — a woman pushing a buggy with a grubby-faced toddler holding on reluctantly as they cross the road; people chatting, walking by. I decide to contact my work colleague, Mary, to see if she can amend and stamp my forms. She and I have developed a friendship over the years and I know she is a place of support whatever the circumstances. I need the sensitive, humane approach and not just another impersonal office. I could make it to meet her and back to the welfare office before they close. Somewhat revived I make the call.

I join Mary in a coffee shop at a local beauty spot where she was meeting an American and an Irish man, both of whom, alongside their spiritual pursuits, have devoted their lives to developing programmes for young people in difficulty in inner-city environments. Always interested in people and finding ways to meet their needs, Mary often goes over and above the call of duty in the workplace. As the conversation unfolds I am invited to join them in a ceremony that is being led by the American. I can't quite understand what they are asking but neither can I believe my ears when he mentions that we would visit a housing estate which, quite incredibly, shared my son's name, Darragh Park. Intrigued, I agree immediately.

And so I find myself standing at the infamous Brigid's Well partaking in a blessing. I am no stranger to such things having spent some years learning spiritual ways under the guidance of a spiritual leader or two. Even by my standards this is surreal. Had I not just left the crazy world of social welfare systems or is this the crazy world? I moved from the impersonal to the inter-connectedness of all things. Incredible as it sounds, my day polarises to the extreme. I find myself dedicating a blessing to all the young people of the town, the county and the country, especially the teenagers. Neither of the men knew my circumstances when they asked me to join them. In fact, they are as astounded as I when the synchronicities come to light. The form filling is forgotten until another day and I drive home lighter and incredulous at how things have materialised. I'm smiling to myself as I think you couldn't make this stuff up.

I return to the social welfare office a few days later with a plan. I play a game of 'Imagine if' while I await my turn. I envision having a bag of money in envelopes and walking up to each person in the line and handing them a large lump sum, inviting them to spare themselves the indignity of that particular line. I imagine offering every worker who feels fed up or burned out in the job a chance to leave. By the time I arrive at the pane of glass I find my interaction is still wobbly and tears are close to the surface but I maintain my composure. Once again I try to convey my circumstances. Success this time! I get a claim processed and thankfully, most weeks, a sum of money would arrive on my mat. This relief was short-lived however, as systems and real life were to clash again and I became no longer entitled to support. Another day's story!

Chapter 7
Are you two a couple?

~

'Are you two a couple?' asks the Polish guy at salsa class. An interesting and simple question but like the other interesting and simple questions such as, 'Do you have children?' my answer is not so simple. I sigh heavily as it certainly doesn't feel like that this evening. The dance teacher has brought roses for all the men to pass to a woman in class for Valentine's Day. It's cheesy to say the least, but when he goes elsewhere with his rose and not to me, I'm really upset.

I know this is because here in this environment he hasn't claimed *us*. In fact outside of *us*, he hasn't claimed us. I answer the Polish guy glibly and gather myself for the next song. The beauty of this class is that it calls for me to be fully there, to remember the steps as I move from man to man. Salsa is fast and really brings me into my body and out of my head. Of course I'm much older than most here, but I am beyond caring; it's good for my mind and body. When he and I have our turn I'm struggling to stay composed. He knows me well; he feels I'm vulnerable. And yet I doubt he will get the why. As he looks at me with questions in his eyes, I fumble over the footwork as tears escape. I'm grateful for the 'change partner' command and stand to face the next guy, with some semblance of composure.

By the end of class, I bolt out first into the cool night air and stand with my back up against a tree. This big old bark supports my back in the middle of the noisy city street where sounds compete loudly with each other and people spill out of the bar next door. It's a weeknight and I'm surprised it is so busy. I wait impatiently for him to appear. It seems to be taking him forever. As soon as he arrives out, he asks what is going on. He is taken aback at my response. 'The rose,' I reply. I am not usually so sensitive or in need of attention in this way. Our relationship is so much deeper and real than a cheesy rose foisted upon the men by the dance teacher. As usual we get to the deeper underlying issue.

Derek is busy for most of the weekend with dance practices. He has been dancing for years now; it's his passion. He has studied many styles and performs occasionally in shows. It is a really important part of his life, I know this. Lately it feels like he has been using it as a barrier to us. In the priority list I feel I'm certainly down the line. He is busy a lot these days. I feel inflamed with power or anger, it's a thin line, and I'm teetering on an edge of something. 'Stop shutting me out! Stop pushing me away! What are you doing? What am I doing? If I didn't come to salsa class would I even see you?' All of this emotive questioning floods out and I'm suddenly exhausted.

He responds. That's not his intention. He hears and understands what I'm saying. He does want to be in this deepened version of us. I know he is speaking from his heart, I can feel it. We have practised a very deep honest way of communicating for many years now as really close friends. He has been my rock through separation and divorce, house moves and relationships. All kinds of issues have been tossed about into the clear space with him. This new departure into partnership scares us both as it changes the goalposts. Can the clear space stay clear? We have so much more invested in this now. It all feels heavy and a lot to process. We head back to his house somewhat resolved to stay alert to speaking out in the moment as much as we can. After a broken sleep beside him I awake with the words, 'It ain't over til it's over,' singing away in my head. I smile at the irony of this. It is early days for all of it.

A few nights later, we are up in the hills walking and the moonlit road looks amazing, as if the light is coming from far beyond the starlit sky that's visible to us. We have had some food and as the weekend draws to a close I wonder what the week will bring. After weeks of pushing me away and pulling me back, right here in this moment we are so connected in love and he has opened his heart a chink more to let that love express itself, across the divide, untainted by fear. Outside the local hardware chain on a Tuesday afternoon, this same feeling of total connectedness between us is reflected in the most ordinary of moments doing the most ordinary of things – buying a tin of paint to paint his bathroom.

His heart has such capacity for love. I am reminded of the ease and resonance that is an instantaneous, tangible feeling of relief in our whole being when we spend time together. That is the way of it between us ever since we first met. It is as if I can draw in a deep breath in his presence and him in mine and that's a discernible feeling that happens spontaneously in each other's company. He described it often as a comfortable old shoe that you just love to slip on. Not exactly a passion enhancer!

The first time our lips met in what we later called 'the kiss that wasn't a kiss' was a surreal experience. Walking in the park, we pause by a tree, the beech tree that becomes a place of refuge for me, and as our lips meet it's as if the whole world turns on its head. The predominant feeling is of reality shifting – time, things, sights, sounds, everything fades into the background and only we exist but we are moving through time. It's a mind-blowing feeling that stays with us for most of the rest of that evening and leaves us speechless for a time as we simply relax and feel it wash over us. In some way, deep in me, I know from that moment that he and I have a purpose of some significance and despite my occasional doubts, that moment and many more since clearly represent a bigger-picture meaning to our lovely connection, and so I hang in there.

Needless to say this pattern emerging from him of closing me out feels so inconsistent with my usual experience of our communication when we were just friends. He is like a rose bud, opening and unfolding until, just as it comes to full beauty and full blossom, it closes itself back to the bud, safely protecting the folds inside. He helps and heals and loves so much. He spends time looking to find answers to the why of things. He feels and interprets energy and is more empathic than most people I know. He helps hundreds of people heal and yet he doesn't clearly see his own patterns. It is fair to say this is not always the case. His fear of being restricted, held back, classified as part of a twosome is splitting his sense of self. His struggle with really letting go of his marriage, now over for a couple of years, is but a sentiment, holding him, entangling him. His awareness of this most vulnerable place that he has ever witnessed in me is blurring the vision. My brokenness has washed away the ground. I'm in a torrential flow, and I'm out of control. He fears he is like a piece of driftwood that I may take hold of and cling to for dear life. Even the possibility of this developing creates fear in him and he backs away. I am a high risk and hurting me would be a catastrophic mess for both of us.

A month passes and the dance continues, the in and out of it, the push and pull of it, pulling me in close and loving me fully then pushing me away. Resembling dance class, he pulls me in, sends me off into a spin and pulls back in close again. Scared of the commitment, he busies himself with stuff to do to impede and distract himself from being too caught up in the relationship – a relationship he is already in, participating in, running away from, loving me in, hiding from me in and hiding from himself in. In some insane way I am so distracted by my flooding of emotions that, for the most part, I stay in an observer consciousness and tell him what I witness – the beauty of our years of friendship.

Exhaustion is a major player in my daily life and some days I am too tired to care about what we are or where we are. I know I can depend on him for support when I'm overwhelmed. Our friendship is intact. No matter what else, he can be there when the deluge hits. The capacity for me to trust and let myself be an emotional mess is not contaminated with any fears or questioning of what we are to be. And so when an opportunity to go away together materialises, without hesitation I say yes, as does he. We begin to plan a trip to the sun in the late summer, an opportunity to embrace and explore the new version of our relationship.

Chapter 8
Time out in Spain

~

I don't know if I've ever felt so loved. Since we arrived in this most beautiful Spanish town of Ayamonte on the Portuguese border, and it is just the two of us, it has been incredible. Love pervades everything we do. The emotional push–pull is now a distant memory. One evening as we walk along the beach by the water's edge, the sky tints in shades of pastel oranges and pinks. We stop in a beachside bar to witness the spectacle. A cherub-like child with a mass of blonde hair clambers up on the wooden rail beside us to get a higher perspective. A child, whose face I never did see, unwittingly brought us both to a higher place of awareness. He perched on his physically elevated viewpoint resonates with me as if on some other level. As the sun makes its descent on the watery horizon, the sound of 'Ave Maria' blasts out of the speakers, timed impeccably by the bar owner who himself is honouring the majesty of this great natural phenomenon that occurs evening after evening.

And here in this heavenly place we have taken the time to stop and watch. No one speaks in the bar as the beach is bathed in effervescent light. Many stand in small clusters, observing from the water's edge. Others sit on soft sand as the day is drawing to a close. I feel privileged to be part of the scene. We watch as many of the families gather in small groups and begin packing up their day's activities. Toddlers run bare-bottomed alongside parents, grandparents, sisters, brothers, aunts and uncles. The sense of family is so palpable. The sight of each person, sun-kissed and bronzed, reduces me to tears of both pain and pleasure. It's as if we have been transported to a place where things look happy, positive and good for all those in our range and viewpoint. Can we shift our perspective to this view at will, I wonder, even if we carry great loss within our hearts? What burdens do those I am observing carry that are not visible to the naked eye? Does waking up to the warm sun and the blue sky feel as delightful when this is the norm for those who live here?

The change of scenery, the change in the weather, the shift in the normal natural triggers has left me feeling more relaxed and at ease, even within the layers of tears and sadness that don't disappear but seem to be less consuming. Like the child on the railing, it's as if I have a different perspective, a slightly elevated viewpoint, from which I can almost observe the wave of emotion as I feel it coming and sometimes even choose not to get submerged by its tumbling, breaking crest. I find myself ever more open to love. The honest, integral, intimate communication that we share is bringing such a feeling of connection to all things, especially nature and family.

It's early evening, and we wander along a beachside path lined with trees and feel the light breeze as it creates a swish in the foliage and a kiss to my face. I feel extremely present to the moment, a feeling that we are growing so much more accustomed to as the week passes. We see things with the newness and freshness of a child, and I can say 'we', as we discuss this quite frequently. After dinner we find a beach walkway hidden by a soft overgrowth of fern and grass-like plants. A lonely gatekeeper asks for a light as we pass him on the wooden bridge and on to the sand. The beach is empty and the sky is laden with stars. A distant glow of ambient light reflects the town's activity.

We stop and sit on the cool sand, held by the magic of the unspoilt space. The love is palpable and almost extraordinary as we embrace and connect. After a time we see someone coming along the water's edge. Larger than life, dressed in white, striding with big regular strides, unwavering as he half-glides-half-walks by. He is tall, very tall, and neither of us speaks as he passes. I am fascinated. I can still see him for quite a time after he passes us by. The feeling is so tangibly clear and magical and serene.

A realisation starts to dawn on us both simultaneously. How is he so visible in the dark from our viewpoint? Is that a male or female? We savour the feeling before getting involved in solving the mystery. Then Derek goes to the water's edge and I cannot see him; he has been absorbed into the darkness and his outline is barely visible. I switch on the torch on my phone and I see him but he is so small. I am dressed in white so he suggests I go to the shoreline. I walk the short distance and find myself spontaneously skipping and dancing and splashing with the freedom of the light breeze I experienced earlier. It's amazing. I am laughing as tears of joy spill down my face. I am calling, 'Can you see me?' I see the torchlight waving around. He is astounded and his laughter joins mine, incredulous and light and joyous. We take some time to realise the probability that we have somehow crossed a veil, as worlds merge for a moment in time. It sounds so extraordinary; it is extra-ordinary. It seems of a supernatural nature.

Have we managed to co-create some grand illusion basked in a glow of love? Are we crazy together in this moment? Does my dead son have anything to do with this? Is there a parallel existence just a hair's breadth away from us on this plane of life? Did that being have any awareness of us? It didn't appear to have flinched as it passed by. I am reminded of a book I read called *The Secret of Shambhala*. It speaks of a heavenly, mythical place way up in the Himalayas near Tibet that only few have accessed. You need to be resonating at a certain vibrational level of consciousness and undergo deep inner changes to access this place where wisdom and insight is kept.

Quantum physics is confirming that we are all energy matter and constantly in flux and change so that we can and do have influence over our domain. As we change our thoughts, we alter the vibrational level of resonance. This brings or attracts more of that frequency to us in daily experience. It's as if we are tuning in to a radio station and as we fine-tune the dial we get clearer reception. From science to popular culture, the laws of the universe are being studied and questioned to unlock our potential and discover our impact on our micro world of cellular development as well as the broader environment and world around us. Feeling good, happy and excited resonates at a faster frequency and generates more good feeling. Feeling negative, despondent and disillusioned creates more bad feeling. This is a truth I've learned. Being down and out brings me into a spiral of negative feeling. When I can turn and find the silver lining, things move in a more positive direction.

Whatever the answer to this surreal experience, it comforts me with a warm glow for the rest of the week and for long months after in a way that's hard to put into words. It's as if our language doesn't have the words to describe the feeling. The duality of agony and ecstasy can best describe the paradoxical nature of my life and the emotions I feel. How can I know such love and live with such pain all in one week, one day, sometimes in one moment? It's a question that continues to intrigue and beguile me over this unfolding journey.

Chapter 9
Joined at the hip

~

One of my inner circle, Audrey, is home from the States with her lovely man. She flew home for the funeral, dropping everything in her Chicago life for a week of supporting me, and now, months later, is here to introduce us to her love. I'm on the way to a restaurant to see her and those solid core friends from college days. We, a group of six women, shared a number of living spaces together throughout college and travelled to the States together, where two remained in residence ever since. Our bond has deepened over the thirty years we have grown, matured, fallen in and out of love, jobs and marriages. We have continued to support each other in real and loving ways through all manner of trials and tribulations.

I pass Darragh's best friend walking alone on our street, head bent, body held tight against the cold. His friendship cut short so harshly, it's more than I can bear to see him alone. They were joined at the hip, one always accompanying the other as the crew gathered for the evening to hang out. I've no doubt he is on his way to one of the others' homes. They travel in a pack but nonetheless a feeling of desolation overwhelms me – mine or his, I cannot be sure. This is so unfair for all of us. I have to pull in. I cannot drive. I'm wracked with grief.

I arrive late for the meal and wonder about the wisdom in being there at all. In some instances this very delicate line between pulling myself out of the feeling enough to be in such company or allowing the full deluge to continue is a tricky one to call. Often I have no choice; tonight I want to see the American contingent so I arrive.

The chic but small French restaurant is bustling with conversation spilling over from one table to the next and into the more general space of the room. Red-checked napkins and wine bottles take precedence in their characteristic French style and chunky wooden tables line the walls. Smells of herbs and baked French rolls accost my senses, even through a sniffly nose.

Audrey jumps up to welcome me and we embrace in a tearful exchange. I meet and chat with her very pleasant partner, Ed. Paula, with her natural sunny disposition, is helping to support me in her warm way. But it's very raw; I spend time trying to engage but I'm not really there. I feel like there's a big gap between me and the experience I see before me. I am trying hard to pull myself together. I push my food around the plate, hardly able to swallow or taste until eventually I retreat to the sanctuary of the bathroom. I come out to find Helen sitting on a stool, waiting patiently. I am struck by the level of strength and support she has as she waits to ask what I would like to do next. It seems as if she is a pillar of strength offered in a way that totally supports me without judgement. That same strength was exhibited the night in our sitting room as she held the notepad and chaired the meeting to arrange his funeral. The same, wonderful friend who called *the meeting about me* — a true diamond of a friend. It's not a difficult choice. I exit early, determined to bring myself home, although many offers of a lift and place to stay are made.

I need to be alone in this rawness, with no witness. This is too enormous for me to bear. This time I need to go it alone. I find this is a pattern with me. I don't like a witness to the deep and raw pain when it comes. I drive home, intermittently stopping to catch my breath, and I'm thankful for the darkness of the countryside and the quiet roads on which I travel. Once inside my own four walls I feel the pain like dark treacle spreading out through the veins, relentless in its purge of any light in its wake, obscuring the view — deadness, dullness pervades the space.

The house sighs — now empty, lonely, devoid of life and light. Life-enhancing sounds are no longer present, save for my tear-stained crumpled self, searching for solace in his pictures lining my walls and shelves. I stand in front of him and I shout to that smiling face through angry hot tears, 'Your mother's pain knows no bounds. It's beyond comprehension. I am falling apart at the seams. I am barely getting through the day. I am hanging here by a thread. I miss you like crazy. What were you thinking? You have torn me inside out. I grew you in me. I nurtured you. I loved you. I grew with you. How can you have done this to me? How can you have been so selfish? Your sister, your father, everyone that knew you is suffering!'

The anger is huge and my body can barely contain this feeling. At the same time exhaustion is overwhelming me as if I'm too tired to fully feel the rage that's swirling in me. I throw a cushion at the wall, almost waiting for him to respond.

He doesn't flinch, his smile the same as it is every day, frozen. I know I am exhausted. I know I am close to an edge of a total spiral down the black hole. I slump on to the couch and pull a blanket over me and drift in and out of a fitful sleep. I feel as if my body and nervous system has been stripped bare, as if all the coating on my muscles and nerves has been peeled back. This is becoming a regular sort of feeling. I know it's because of the deluges of emotions that hit me. I know the stages of grief. I have been discussing them at work with students for years. I didn't realise how hard and fast they can come, how in one day I can move from denial to anger to acceptance. These stages are fluid and in the moment if I can acknowledge the feeling and let it through, I know I am doing OK. This particular evening, not for the first time or the last, I'm on the floor with it all. I need time to rest, regroup.

I awake the next morning sore and raw and I find myself saying, 'He's not gone. He has transformed and I am learning new ways to relate to him.' It's like I'm saying it whilst wondering where such a sentence came from. It's almost as if I didn't think it. It was just there in my mind waiting for me. I walk around the place all day repeating this phrase and it's working. I feel mildly better about things. I understand positive affirming is good for us to reprogramme our negative conditioned beliefs. I believe when you can get into the feeling of them there is power in that, changing the vibration to help feel better. From where I was the evening before to this new easier place is a welcome move in a better direction, however it comes to be. I am used to writing a list of affirmations relating to various things in my life, yet this particular sentence feels more potent, like it came from another place, like the songs that come sometimes as I awake and move into a day, setting a tone. Whatever it is, it's a shift into a more positive thought and feeling, and I am grateful. I know today is going to be OK.

Chapter 10
Birthday in Budapest

~

A feeling of gratitude fills me once again for my amazing friends. The ease with which we relate, the deep bond that exists without effort, the trust and relaxation that's there, effortlessly born of all our shared years. There's no competition; we are who we are and without judgement, we help each other to be who that is. We know it is a gift and we don't take it for granted.

I'm lying in bed in Mary-Pat's home and this feeling is a residue of a lovely dinner here together. This time I manage to be more present and can participate more fully in the conversation that flows so easily. The room with a warm cosy bed, in a clear, crisp, newly painted space, feels cocoon-like. Mary-Pat's creativity spills out into the quirky, deliberately chosen and well-placed objects and décor. Paint, music, healing all come naturally to this woman who, in recent times, has built an amazing centre called Croí Anú for healing through the arts and sound, in her home place of Moone.

A shiver runs along my spine like a trickle of water and I feel my hair move. It is really tangible. It's him; I know it's him. The room seems brighter. I want it again and stronger. This doesn't happen and I'm trying not to be disappointed. 'There is no separation,' I tell myself as I know he is trying to show me through feeling. I realise that I tend to feel this more when I am in a space of love and gratitude and not in devastation. I wish I could have him at will, where I could just close my eyes and call him in and feel him immediately. I lie awake wondering about this possibility for me.

Do some people already have that kind of relationship with their loved ones who have passed on? Is that the gift a medium has or a skill learned? I drift off into a dream of a lovely, rainbow-coloured sky, the outline of another planet appears, so beautiful and clear. In this dream, I am texting people to tell them to look up at the sky to share this magic, when I see him, floating by, looking at me as if from a photograph. It feels magical, but he is flat, almost two-dimensional, as if we are in a cartoon. I want him to stop and talk to me.

The sound of a loud gale blowing a plastic container outside awakens me. I revel in the imagery of the dream and try my best to recreate it and fall back into it, but sleep escapes me now and by morning I feel raw and devastated. I spent the rest of the darkness asking to see him, feel him, have him back just long enough for a hug, a chat, a something. When morning dawns and the house comes to life, I take myself down the hall towards the kitchen, following the wafting smell of bacon and toast. As I near the door I hear a burst of laughter and I hastily retreat to the bedroom to regroup. I know in this space with these friends that it is OK not to be OK, but I am tired of myself being like this and wonder if I should stay home more. After a bit more self-talk I make myself presentable enough to have a quick chat, and with a piece of toast with melted butter in hand, which their little dog barks hopefully at, I exit quickly and without incident. I don't want to extinguish the sound of laughter.

I take myself home, and as the day unfolds, exhaustion and rawness are my overriding feelings. This roller coaster of emotions renders me exhausted a lot of the time. It's one of those days where just surviving the onslaught is achievement in itself. There are many more of those days it seems, as time goes by, but so far I have a capacity to ride the waves. I wonder if this is the depression stage of grief, the one that saps energy so that nothing feels like it will change the feeling.

My sister, Louise, comes to meet me that evening, as she often does, to check in and cook something lovely. Cooking comes so naturally to her. My interest in such things has waned dramatically. Despite her busy and successful work life, cooking is one of her pleasures and talents and something she makes time to enjoy. Over the course of the evening, she shares with me 'her excellent idea' to bring me away to a secret location for my birthday. Always on the lookout for ways to support, it is a strong characteristic of her personality to want to help or fix things whenever possible. Over the years she has dreamt up many wonderful thoughtful ideas and plans to support and bring fun into our lives, and she has the Midas touch, bringing success wherever she goes. Excitable and enthusiastic by nature, her exuberance is infectious. Many a Christmas morning she would blast a whacky Christmas tune as loud as our sound system could take, exciting already adrenalin-fuelled younger ones about the joy of celebrating as a family.

She suggests I ask Derek to join us. He feels it is not for him to come and so, undeterred, she suggests we ask if one or more of the inner circle might like to come. No hesitation exists with the women and so the conspiracy begins in earnest as they plot and plan and arrange details, none of which I am privy to. I'm encouraged to relax, let go, not worry over any costs or expenses and I will be informed of the type of attire needed for a weekend. Once again I have been asked to hand over the reins of my life to others and the higher intelligence. For a woman of such independence, hardwired to do things for myself, I find this both refreshing and totally challenging. I'm happy to be going away, but I would like to be making my own contribution financially. It's completely astounding, the array of wonderful things my siblings and friends are continuously coming up with, to surprise and support me. I know I am very privileged in the calibre of people I have around me. They are good to the core. In the months since his passing, ironically I've never been so broke or away so often. The paradox of life again. The weekend arrives and Derek drives us to the airport. Budapest turns out to be the destination.

We have an amazing time exploring the city under the guidance of Louise, who has what seems like an incredible knowledge, having visited on a work venture. The city, bisected by the river Danube, is an architectural paradise with magnificent bridges, a plethora of walkways, artisan cafés and 'ruin bars', which are hip and trendy bars converted from old storage warehouses. Probably the most famous attractions are the hot baths that are dotted all over the city. We attend one of the thermal hot baths one sunny afternoon. The place is alive with families and gatherings of people of all genders and ages, all in bathing costumes, hanging out on the patio areas around each pool. Big pillars of concrete surround the natural healing hot waters like something out of a Roman movie. Many of these ancient baths date back to the sixteenth and seventeenth centuries. The feeling of history is palpable. We find a space to lay out our towels and sit and observe the terrain and the people around us for a short time before dipping our bodies into the wonderful warm waters. A sense of heat and relaxation permeates every cell as we immerse ourselves in the water. In one of the whirlpools I find myself laughing out loud as I'm whisked into the vortex of moving water and my feet are off the ground. I feel alive and excited and full of joy. When I put my feet down it stifles and staggers the movement. What a metaphor for life!

I get it! In that moment I get it more than ever I get it. Let go and flow with the energy. I've been attending workshops and listening to enlightened beings telling me this for years. That whirlpool showed me. I got spat out a few times, laughing as I tried to get my bearings. Again this is part of the cycle and whirl of life. I observed people trying to go against the flow and the struggle that ensued. How often have I done that, trying to push against the tide only to exhaust myself?

It's a simple thing I have found so hard to do in the past. I was out there getting stuff done, making stuff happen, until he blew all of it away. Listen and learn to tune into the energy and it will all flow so easily and with fun and adventure. As I write this now, I realise I've been staggering and dispersing the flow. I'm trying to find work to generate income, to get stuff done, and the truth is the energy is here now, on this page, writing. But my mind doesn't trust this. I have no money. I'm living off my friends and family. I need to get out there and make something happen.

Meanwhile back in Budapest, it's the day of my birthday. We go to a café of magnificent proportions, a throwback to times of great opulence. Its marbled walls, high ceilings and gold-embossed pillars have us reeling in its decadent, almost vulgar, display of wealth and grandeur. A pianist plays the theme song from 'Love Story' and some of us wipe a tear from our eyes. I feel Darragh is behind this, bringing me to a place of such contrast to my life's experience at home. He is in the music, he is in the expression of wealth and he is in the support I feel around me. We have an abundant brunch and I feel held in love and celebration.

As we meander through the streets, I find myself again submerged in a wave of grief. A family walk in front of us, a mother and two teenagers or so it looks to me – a tall fair-haired guy with a striped hooded top and a smaller dark-haired girl in jeans and a pink T-shirt. They could be us, our little trio of a family. Once again the flood gives no warning. It holds me to ransom, and I struggle to find a place to sit while my two sentries guard me. As Helen and Mary-Pat wordlessly munch and crunch on their ice cream cones, it seems too ridiculous for words – me, sitting in despair between these two who are engaging in a most inane activity. All of us are conscious of each other and they hold me in the space between them with such strength – without words, without touch, between bites. The city street is bustling with people walking by our little threesome. Conversations fill the air in a language our ears are unaccustomed to. It strikes me that crying has no linguistic distinction that's tangible to the untrained ear. Anyone in that crowd might sound universal in their sobs. Business people, clad in refined clothes, purposeful in their demeanour and deep in discussion walk by. Do they cry much or often? Families are meandering casually along, stopping and starting, looking into shop windows, moving in tandem.

My senses can take all this in whilst the tears flow and the feelings spill out. We wait until it's passed. The signal comes from me to move. As I stand up on shaky legs I can re-engage, albeit in a more subdued manner, with the rest of the day's activities. We meet up with the rest of our entourage and partake in a pleasant evening of dining and music in this city of history. Another milestone achieved, I got through my birthday and with a combination of laughter and tears I find myself so grateful again for my network of support in friends and family.

Chapter 11
Inquest

A call comes during work and at lunch I listen to the message. It's the local Garda and he wants me to make a statement in preparation for the inquest. I cannot believe what is being required of me. I have to present at the garda station and tell them about the last interaction I had with my son. Immediately I feel under suspicion and judged, and I haven't even called the station back to make an appointment. I am stunned, and I feel like I have been sideswiped with a hammer.

How could I not know this was coming, having worked in social care? Yet it is such a bolt out of the blue. I have to walk outside and breathe in some air. I stand in the garden that my team-building class constructed last year. A dynamic and determined group, they worked hard. We had fun, learned so much, laughed, resolved conflicts and made magic as we dug, sowed seeds, planted and transformed a piece of rough ground into a lovely space where now the leaves rustle in the wind as I stand looking for solace. A place of peace was their intention – a place to come and sit with friends or on your own when you needed space. After my son's passing, they called it 'Darragh's Garden'.

I decide to ring back immediately, feeling that if I give this time and headspace I will be a basket case by the end of the working day. The Garda can see me on my way home from work. He knows it is a very sensitive issue and asks if I would prefer him to come to my home. I could not even conceive of that possibility, not even for a moment. His uniformed presence in our home is more than I could bear to repeat. I am assured it is routine and won't take long, and I can bring someone for moral support.

For some reason I am determined to get this over with as quickly as possible and arrange to go directly after work. I am grateful for the nature of my work that afternoon and as I sit with students, discussing the stages of development over a lifespan, I keep thoughts of the impending meeting at bay. The short drive to the station has me less able to escape. I feel guilty that my son disappeared and I ask myself what else I could have done. They need to satisfy themselves that there was no negligence on my part and yet that's all I feel, totally incompetent and negligent. I wasn't able to stop that awful outcome. He carried out the suicide I hadn't even seen or felt was there. I work with energy. I feel things with people. I sense things and help them accordingly and yet I missed this glaring hole with my own flesh and blood.

I try to pull every available tool that years of personal development has given me out of the bag. Stay in the moment! Look and see what's around you! Try not to feed the beast of thought that has been unleashed! But unleashed it is, the thoughts that flood me with every possible negative slant imaginable. I have myself arrested and in jail by the time I park the car. Maybe I should have brought support. I take a deep breath and head in to the station.

Inviting is not the word that comes to mind as I make myself known at the desk. A rather tired, old, clean but dingy décor resonates with my negative thought process. The Garda involved appears, a grim smile on his face. I feel a lurch of pain as I recognise him from that fateful morning. We walk along a small corridor and I muse over the strange circumstances under which we have met. I wonder if he likes this job. He ushers me into a room for our private conversation. Again the sludge-coloured walls and metal furniture brings the feeling of discomfort to an already difficult situation. The metal-framed chair grinds on the floor as I pull it out from the table to sit. I wonder if this uncomfortable furniture was planned in the design of a police station.

He takes out a pen and paper. Although I know this is how this works, I find it almost amusing in such an age of technology that a handwritten report is what the law-enforcing officers deem best practice. He uncomfortably shuffles in his seat as he clears his throat and begins to talk me through what needs to happen. I barely hear a word. We both just want to get this over with. He asks me to describe my last interaction with him, my teenage son. I manage to tell him again what happened. He writes as I speak through a lump in my throat, choking my words as I recall that evening – his last conversation with me, our unsuccessful attempts to reach him, the cold night closing in, praying he was hanging out on someone's couch, all the while knowing this was really out of character for him.

I'm looking at the bent head of the Garda as his writing seems to drag time into slow motion, and I will him to be finished so I can get out and run away as fast as I can. I hear an occasional fleeting conversation as it passes the door. I look around, waiting for his head to lift, to bring his face back into view. The window seems to be made of smoky plastic with a mesh covering outside. Does Kildare need that much protection? Are there hardened criminals in this area who have sat in this metal chair being interviewed? I muse while I wait. We eventually get to the end and he asks if I have any questions. 'When can we have his phone back?' I ask in anticipation. 'When can we have the note hastily written in a blue copybook that had his name neatly printed on the front?'

I saw the copybook and the note on the day we found him. It was rolled up in his coat pocket and the Garda held the page open for us to read. My voice is cracking now as the memory of those words, scrawled on a page, were held in front of me. Darragh's writing reflecting the pace of his mind, badly formed letters spilling out faster than his hand could keep up. I know it told me nothing that helped. He loved us; he named me, his dad and his sister, and was sorry. He had to do it, he said. He had no choice. What does that mean? How could he have felt he had no choice? I still ponder this. 'Tell my friends I love them and I hope they have a good life.' Have a good life without him? What was he thinking? He formed the very fabric of our lives.

I had practically memorised the note in the few hasty minutes of reading it at the scene, but still I craved to have that copybook and his phone. In fact anything belonging to him has been elevated to very important status from my standpoint.

I can see this interview is challenging for this officer. He has teenagers himself he told me that day we found Darragh, that Sunday morning when this man and I first met. I can see him sitting on my couch in his uniform, with a little black notebook in his hand as he asks us a few questions: When did we last see him? What time did we last try to call him? Had we spoken to anyone else who saw him that evening after my last chat with him? Did we notice anything unusual in the days or hours prior to his disappearance?

He tells me now that I cannot have the phone until after the inquest, as they are trying to unlock it for any clues or evidence. The code I have is incorrect. The note also is regarded as necessary to keep in evidence. He is as kind as he can be in trying to explain these rules and precautions to me. I feel a sense of overwhelm lurking within me, and I am getting close to having to take my leave. They will let me know a date for the inquest hearing. In a sudden outburst, I desperately need to ask, 'Do I have to be there? Can they not just send me the autopsy report? Do I have to give evidence? Will his sister have to take the stand? Surely they could not ask her to do that?' A barrage of questions spills out of me, falling over each other as they land into the air between us.

Again the laws of the land are explained to me with patience and tenacity as if I were a small child needing help with my homework. I can feel the burden on him as he explains in a kind but taut voice, intermittent heavy sighs breaking the flow of his explanation. 'It is the procedure, the protocol that has to be followed. Yes, you will have to take the stand to verify the information in this statement. No, his sister will not need to give evidence,' he says.

I get to that point beyond caring. It's time to get out of there. Hastily I stand up, pushing the chair back in one noisy cumbersome move. And so I blunder my way through the corridor, out the door and into the carpark. The solace and privacy of my car allows me the space to fall apart once again before heading home to the lifeless, lonely house that once was a home.

A couple of weeks later I am at the airport feeling the excitement that imminent arrival and travel brings. I am not actually going anywhere. We are dropping a friend off and Derek and I stay to have a coffee and enjoy the atmosphere. It's something we like to do if we get the opportunity. We are having fun imagining where we might like to be going when my phone rings. It's the coroner's office telling me that the inquest will have to be postponed as one of the personnel involved with our case has taken long-term sick leave.

It's amazing how the light-hearted ambience takes a dramatic turn. This act of my son has reared its head again and taken a moment of joy away from me. There is no escape from this. I never know what might open the sluice gate in any moment, on any day. This reality I am now living is inescapable. The fact that the inquest has been postponed calls for relief and yet I feel quenched of life in the moment. Moving it out three months more! Three months of trying not to think or worry about that day or what outcome it will bring.

Will he have a substance in his blood? Would it be better for him if he was under the influence of alcohol or drugs, so he was out of his mind and could feel little or no pain, his sister and I sometimes wonder. What would that say about us the parents? Three months to find out what time of the night he died at, and whether or not he suffered? Would any or all of those questions be answered?

It's nearly ten months after he died before we get to the inquest. How does one face this kind of an event? I find as the time approaches, I repeatedly wonder at the madness of having a day in court to trawl through the details of his untimely passing. It feels almost too difficult to bear. My little experience of court, with divorce and occasional work-related appearances, renders me ever more apprehensive – the clinical, cold, academic language; the sense of ritual and ceremony alien to most people; the insensitive nature of the proceedings as people's trauma and life experiences become files with a case number.

Derek and I spend the night before in front of the fire, in a cocooned feeling, fanned by the orange–red glow of the flames. The warm, safe atmosphere in the room is far removed from the events about to unfold. Intermittent sleep is as good as it gets and as the day dawns I call on

Darragh to come and support us all. 'You better be there and hold us together for this,' I say, wondering at my own madness as I speak to him in this way. We arrive at the courthouse and I am pleasantly surprised to see some close friends and family waiting. Other families, taut and grim-faced, gather. We are all suffering the same atrocity. Someone tries to ascertain how the morning will proceed. The tiled foyer of the courthouse is filled with a strange hush, yet strands of tense and uncertain conversation hang in the air. A courtroom door opens and all are ushered inside to be seated on the hard pew-like benches.

The courtroom layout is according to hierarchy – the judge's wooden pulpit box; the witness stand; the jury box, today inhabited by uniformed Gardaí associated with cases. All of us, the families in pain all together at the end of the room, seated like obedient children waiting to find out what lies in store. All rise as the judge presiding enters. An explanation of the day's events follows and a lengthy long-winded account of the constitutional purpose of inquest is read. I sit in agonising impatience for this to be over and done. I can hardly take in a word of what is being said. There may be members of the public and possibly members of the media present, I do hear that. Beside me Ciara sits, her young face tense and fraught with stress. I strain to keep thoughts of her life experience in this moment at bay as tears here feel futile and almost unbecoming, as if that matters.

The tension in the room is palpable as if the collective are holding their breath in dread. A list of cases is called in the order they are to be heard. We are fourth on the list and should be heard by lunchtime. I am slammed into reality just hearing his name read out in court. We have to wait a couple more hours to be awakened from this particular nightmare. We are advised to take time out down town.

Outside the courthouse I get to greet the Garda I have been engaging with. He, it transpires, was the person on extended sick leave as his brother fatefully also ended his life in suicide a few weeks after our last meeting. I hardly know what to say to this man, who is holding his professional boundary as tears flicker in his eyes. We speak in an unspoken language: 'I know you are in pain and I wish you did not have to do this today as do you!' It's as if my mind is speaking to him silently. How can we explain this craziness that is infecting our society today? My young son, his middle-aged brother, the list in the courthouse to be heard just this day! I'm shook even more by the encounter with this Garda, and shakily, I walk to a nearby café.

I frequent this place often, but today our solemn little party and I are in such a different reality to the other customers. I feel like an alien on a day excursion to earth to observe human habits as the ordinary life of this street and café seem miles away from me. I do catch the swaying of the autumn-coloured boughs right outside the window where I am sitting; nature for a moment saves me in its eloquent grace of letting go. Leaves change and gently fall away, allowing the tree to nourish itself for regrowth. We are trying to do the same but today this is so far from possible. This day in court opens up the wound and squeezes until you cry out in pain. Of course, that's not evident as I sit sipping tea with my closest family and friends, waiting for the time to pass so our turn can be over.

I barely remember the walk back to the courthouse. I feel shaky from head to toe, yet I can walk and talk. We are seated and the judge is kind and considerate as he reminds us of procedure. The coroner's report is read. A lot of it is meaningless but toxicology comes back negative. There's no trace of alcohol or drugs in his blood. My mind does a double backflip. Oh no! He was in his right mind, he must have felt everything and how could that be? And at the same time I am feeling that is good, he wasn't off his head. The judge asks if we have any questions. Gregg asks for time of death and I am relieved someone thought to ask that. Unfortunately they could not ascertain it and I feel disappointment flood through me. It's immaterial at this point but I want to know. Next, the Garda reads his report: there was nothing on his phone that would give cause for concern. Then I am called to the witness stand.

As if in slow motion, I stand and walk up through the courtroom. Standing in the box, I see the faces of our beloved, those who love me and him, sitting stony-faced watching me, willing me to be strong and brave, supporting me. My statement is read. It sounds vaguely familiar. I remember the day in the station sitting with the Garda giving that statement. A couple of sensitively asked questions from the judge follow: Did I give that statement willingly? Is there anything I would like to add? I am dismissed and walk quietly, stifling sobs, back to my space on the pew. Dave then has to follow suit. The judge gives some more information which I cannot hear as I am openly sobbing now. I cannot contain it anymore. The sombre crew of support now begin to show cracks in their demeanour. Darragh's sister, my sister, my father and brothers, my partner and friends – each in their own way grappling with their individual emotional spillover as the court proceedings draw to a close.

He is legally recorded as death by his own volition and we can leave. I am anxious to get his belongings back. The Garda meets me at the door of the courtroom and wants to speak to me discreetly. There seems to be an issue with the blue copybook as some lewd drawing was present on the first few pages. I am almost amused at the serious nature of his tone and how the judge has deemed it necessary to remove those pages.

'What?' I ask. 'The penis drawings? Is that what you are referring to?'

'Yes,' he replies, 'I'm afraid it seems the judge regards that material as too sensitive to return to you.'

I am half annoyed at the arrogance of such a choice being made for me. Even if it is the judge, he is not the parent of the dead teen who drew penises on a page and neither was my teenage son the first to graffiti such things in an unused copybook. Battle-weary, I make my dissatisfaction known but decline to complain more formally. I am more interested in rereading the note that remains unaltered in the shamed copybook. The note that felt like it was of such earth-shattering significance is read and reread by most of our group. I watch as their faces crumple as they read words that say so little in the face of such enormity.

Ciara walks with me the short distance back to the car and describes almost an identical reaction to the toxicology report as I have – a simultaneous feeling of relief and disappointment. She is bearing up well under the strain and I would give anything to spare her this, yet I have no way of saving her from the gross impact of her brother's actions. I feel helpless as a parent as I watch her struggle to come to terms with this new life that he foisted upon us. I see my own parents wrestle with their own pain and helplessness around me; it's a domino effect.

Seeing your offspring in pain and feeling helpless in the midst of this is a difficult road to walk. Darragh's artist impressions do create a ripple of laughter as the word gets around our little enclave of teary-eyed, emotionally threadbare warriors, that the pages were removed from the copybook. He always loved a laugh and at times it's hard to muster up the enthusiasm to laugh, but it serves us all very well in this moment. The gravity of the inquest is lightened by a couple of badly drawn penises. He has got to be behind this, laughing out loud, if only I could hear him.

We arrive at my parents' house to debrief. My anxious mother and Lisa, my sister's partner, have been waiting there with bated breath to hear the outcome. As we arrive en masse and voices drown out the silence, the chatter starts and relief is tangible. Another milestone has been reached. Ciara stays but a short while and leaves with her boyfriend Kevin. I last only a short while longer before I signal Derek. We are leaving and driving to a nice hotel by the coast to recuperate and recover after the day. I embrace the sadness once again in the comfort and anonymity of his car as he drives and I play back the events in my mind and let the feelings wash over me.

Chapter 12
A return to birth

I wake up shouting Darragh's name with no idea why. No dream fragment lingers to explain this audible cry that disturbed my sleep. The level of desperation that follows is tantamount to a bulldozer in a field of poppies, as the emotions rage through me, stripping my body and soul. I allow it to subside, check the clock and head for the bathroom.

An unrecognisable version of me stares back from the mirror. This sad, tired, shallow face can't be me, can it? It's almost a year since he left and I'm not sure when this face changed. It has crept up on me whilst I worked so hard at getting through this storm, the tornado tearing my life from its roots, which clearly has ravaged my body as well as my emotions. Not renowned for being good at self-care, is this now the payback of my slovenly ways – that wizened, crumpled and deeply lined face? Not with 'life-enhancing map of the wonderful life I've lived' lines but rather a reflection of stress, hard work and finally the shattering effect of his suicide. I feel so much. I ride the waves of emotion, picking up the surfboard every time I crash and roll. But it's taking its toll. Gone is the little pleasure I had in looking more youthful than my years, gone into an acceleration forward in time written all over my face and woven in my body. Is there no end to the damage his selfishness caused? Given that the inquest is only over and his first birthday since he left looms, it's hardly a wonder; nonetheless it is a shock to behold.

An hour later the morning routine ensues and the road to work is paved with a dance around the edge of exhaustion and tears. The week unfolds with various degrees of pain as the birthday comes closer. Dave's house is to be the venue, where a bonfire they constructed for last Halloween had never got ignited. It feels fitting that this transpires in his father's; their relationship, often fraught with tension in recent times, had begun to heal. The birthday morning dawns and I awake with a song in my head, a regular occurrence in my life since his passing. This one is a reflection of my insecurity. The words pound in my head: 'How can I protect you in this crazy world?' It stirs me up emotionally and I am grateful not to be working today. Ciara, Louise and I are spending the day together.

In the general getting ready for the day, I am astounded to find that I seem to have a period. I am almost incredulous as no hint of one has been evident since his passing and now today physiologically my body remembers his birthday. This day, sixteen years ago, I gave birth to him, a beautiful bundle of hope and potential who was to conquer the world and fulfil many dreams. This version of events was not the anticipated outcome.

I know it's a long day yet, and I try not to indulge these feelings, so I make the necessary adjustments to my attire and go downstairs to meet the women. This physiological remembering is still foremost in my thoughts. Ciara wants to go to the grave. It's not a place I frequent often. In fact I rarely visit, as often it takes days to recover. I don't feel he is there but the starkness of some overturned soil and adornments from his friends breaks my heart even more. That and seeing a similar scene two graves away — football jerseys, photos and coloured rubber wristbands neatly arranged — as another teenager is remembered by his family and friends. A woman that I have never met in this small town suffers the same fate as me. Our sons knew each other, sat together in woodwork class. Her son left six months before mine. I used to often wonder how she managed to face another day and now I am her.

We arrive at the graveside, his little birthday crew. Ciara carries the helium balloon with 'Happy 16th Birthday' printed across it, she insists it is a requirement on this day. Our family was good for birthdays. A day to celebrate you was encouraged and children's parties were a regular occurrence in our home as they grew. I returned home on my birthday just months before he left to find my bedroom filled with colourful balloons. Darragh and Ciara had blown them up and decorated every space available to them, making my bed resemble a bag of jellybeans. This day last year I had him and his crew in the car heading off to the south of Dublin where they battled in fun at a paintball facility, filling the journey home with stories of battle strategies and counting wounds with their usual exuberance.

I marvel at Ciara's strength. I'm not so sure I can manage to deal with the reality that today brings. We drive the short distance to the graveyard. Louise is at the wheel, knowing we may all need some crying time. My heart lurches as I am faced with his piece of ground, tidy and flower-filled by the kind-hearted, broken-hearted mother of one of his crew. She is a youth club leader and saw him that last day as he and a few of the crew were helping with the Santa's grotto preparation. She knows I cannot deal with the grave and has taken it upon herself to tend to it. She also knows that funds to pay for the plot are proving really hard to come by and so she has taken it upon herself, with the help of her husband and some youth club leaders, to organise a fundraiser memorial to cover this cost. The gratitude that floods me is hard to express. Often fanciful imaginings have me arriving at her door and the doors of many others with some momentous gesture of a gift of thanks to show my appreciation for the kindnesses she and many like her have bestowed upon me and my daughter.

Back in the graveyard we spend time all in our own feelings. I am deeply submerged in devastation. 'How can I protect you in this crazy world?' still echoes in my head and the feeling that I didn't is predominant. We leave in silence and return to the house to make tea – an extraordinary Irish ritual that fixes anything and is appropriate at every event. Feeling in observer mode I see the strain on Louise's face, her grief taking a different route to mine. Her busy life schedule doesn't leave much space for grief. Her last encounter with him was the dinner before her big trip to Australia as a celebration of her civil partnership with Lisa, a major milestone for them as a couple and a follow-up to their big day out a few months prior. The family had gathered to send them off and he came with his close mate and childhood friend. None of us knew what would occur a little over a week later.

His crew gather at our house later in the day. They had been at school – a jolt to my being that life carries on and they still attend school, even on their dead friend's birthday. Instead of the health warnings about drinking and behaving badly, this gathering is more solemn yet alive in its cluster of male hormones. Ciara, Louise and I ferry them over to the celebration of sorts. The weather is dry but crisp, and a big pot of food cooked by Dave and his partner Sinead is welcomed and devoured by the crew as we sit in the garden. Darragh's light-filled little brother, Cillian, fuelled by enthusiasm for life, runs to greet me and his sister Ciara, his face alive with warmth and love. Darragh's childhood friend meets us here; his parents are friends of mine since our teens. This has impacted hugely on their lives too as our children grew up together. The gathering is a strange mix of family and friends, and we sit around a firepit.

In days of old, some of this same collection of people would have sat at campfires in our garden. Dave is a master of firepits and barbecues. The kids' childhood friends would enjoy campouts in the garden with stories and marshmallows around the fire for many summers. It strikes me that fire is playing an important role in this evening. His crew have wandered down the large field-like garden to the bonfire. Leftover fireworks have been brought to mark the occasion. We trickle our way down to the fire ceremony as loud sparkles momentarily light up the sky. My body is so tightly wound it feels taut and might break in two.

Ciara stands, her arms wrapped around Cillian. What will he remember of his older brother, gone from him when he was only three years old? The night Darragh left this world that same child called his nanny to the window to come and look at Darragh outside the window with the light. The dilemma the whole funeral posed to this young child's parents. Dave, ripped apart by his older son's sudden departure from the world, wanting to protect his younger son, sent him to his nanny's, away from the intense grieving. He sees light not grief! Can he see him now? I wonder. Do they converse? Does such a young pure spirit have more instantaneous access across the divide? Ciara tells me earlier in the evening he came tugging at her to come over to the side of the house as there was a man in white clothes who wanted to see her. No such person was there when they arrived.

The large flames of the bonfire begin to lick the darkness and in brief moments one or other of his crew resemble him so much. It takes all my strength not to cry out my pain. I wonder at the wisdom of not having Derek here and I vow to ask for his support in future in such things. Meanwhile, Darragh's crew and childhood friend stand in small clusters around the flames, chatting and feeding the fire as the flames expand and wane. Then it's time to send the lanterns into the sky. My smiles are more like grimaces, as in twos and threes we try to get the paper lights fuelled, lit and ready for take-off. As they make their way into the starlit sky, my sense of him and his journey to the beyond comes to mind. A resounding hush falls on the scene as his most loved and loving of him pause to watch their journey. This feels like a fitting celebration for him. I can feel the change in the crew and friends as these majestic lights are taken by the wind far into the great beyond. It's poignant, stark, beautiful and painful. 'Happy birthday wherever you are,' I whisper on to the wind. I wait with Ciara until the last trace of the last lantern disappears into the night before returning to the gathering and taking ourselves home.

Chapter 13
Memorial: remembering with
ancestors

Barely time to catch my breath and it's his anniversary. As if we need reminding; or anyone associated with us we have that date etched forever in our minds. However, it is a good opportunity to remind ourselves of all the joy and pain he brings us and has done over the past years.

This is daily practice for me at least; maybe for others this is a chance to stop and take stock of the year just passed. Anniversary — another of those societal rituals that previously passed me by without much thought. My closest family and friends were still part of my life, still living, breathing souls partaking in the human experience. Therefore no need for deep scrutiny of such things evolved for me. Now that need feels great. How best to honour him? I appreciate the support and certainty that the Catholic ritual provides in these instances. The mass, the priest remembering the loved one, suffices as a focal point of the anniversary. We on the other hand are creating it as we go, intuition playing the leading role in decisions.

Ideas for the day flow fairly naturally. An open invitation to the Hill of Tara on the day seems most fitting as all of us, including Darragh, have an affiliation with that place. The evening before is the memorial event in the local GAA hall. Once again the youth club leaders take this event in hand. There are some people in this world who have a way of pre-empting others' needs and going all out to be supportive.

This small town youth club are remarkable in their response to these tragedies in their community. A large support resource for young people in the area, they magnify their time and energy and multiply their resources to hold and help the youth affected by this act of his.

The ripples of such things reach way beyond my conscious awareness as is reflected in the deluge of cards and written letters received in the months after. A young teen from another local town wrote: 'You don't know me. I knew him to see. I have a disability and school was difficult for me but Darragh always took time to talk to me. I'm so sad he is gone.' A mother tells me she has had fears of her daughter's depression and that this could have been her story but somehow the impact of his act has helped her teen open up, speak about her feelings and seek help. The young people are shouting loudly for us to pay attention in our society. How can we honour and respect their development as they navigate the choppy waters of adolescence? How can we help them develop confidence, resilience and communicative skills, especially in the area of emotional expression? What can we do as a society, as a school system and as parents? So many unanswered questions fill my mind regularly.

It transpires that the event is a showcase for young local bands and is perfect, as music always featured largely in our home. Decisions are run past us in a sensitive, caring way. All teens and children can enter free of charge and the tickets are sold at a small fee of €5 to adults. Ciara invests herself in this project and asks local businesses to donate prizes for the raffle. It is paying dividends in many ways. She describes feeling good in having a focus that relates to him and gets her doing something. This turns out to be a theme for her as she involves herself in another project in a Youth Garda Diversion Programme whereby they use our family story to make a short film to encourage young people to ask for help as: 'Help is There'. This they hope can be used as a teaching aid in schools locally and perhaps even countrywide.

And so with little or no effort on my behalf, a truly amazing evening unfolds. An offer from a couple of more accomplished bands to perform draws a large youth presence. First up is one of his crew, Shaun Doyle, an up-and-coming artist, for sure. This is his first formal gig and he has worked hard preparing loops and mixes to accentuate his performance. He is blessed with natural talent so this results in a stunning performance. Singer and songwriter, he plays a song he penned and dedicated to his good friend called 'Summer Time', describing how he'd give anything for another summer with him. I'm standing at the side of the stage swelling with pride and sadness in the same moment. He calls on the crew to come and perform as they did for me, that very poignantly worded song called 'Timshel' by Mumford and Sons.

I wonder did the writer of those particular lines have any idea how relevant to our circumstances this has become. In fact, most of that album featured in some way in our lives. He and I both loved and listened to it regularly; his crew practised lyrics and music from it; songs featured at his funeral sending a message that 'love will not break your heart', a sentiment we would defy in our experience.

Some of the crew are shy and not ready to be on stage in front of an audience. His joined-at-the-hip friend, in particular, is reticent and the others ask me to help cajole him. I am mindful he is in a room of peers and adults and don't want to put him under too much pressure but this is important, and so playfully and with some emotional charge I ask and he concedes.

To hear those voices of his nearest and dearest sing in harmony together, words that are so emotive and beautiful and so reflective of their own experience, is something that stays with me ever since that first performance in my sitting room. The underlying message is 'Death will steal your innocence but not your substance, you are not alone in this, together we will stand.' I feel ripples of energy like cold breezes all over my body. The room is captivated, a message is coming through. Love for these strong, brave, amazing teenagers floods me and he, smiling from the projected images covering the wall, looks on.

Teens get a bad rap in my view.

In the break between bands, friends and family chat, mingle and eat sandwiches; the teenagers slip outside for a smoke or a catch up. My siblings and close friends have developed good relationships with his crew, especially over the events of the last year. The atmosphere is easy as people intermingle, swap stories and pause to look at himself in many moments of his teenage life. Cocktail sausages and sandwiches are passed around on trays and teas and coffees seem more popular than the alcohol that is served. Children hop and skip between stools and dance on the large floor space in front of the stage. The main attraction, the 'Valentine Blacks', get the teens back in place and the room is rocking. These are followed by 'The Spirit Merchants', 'The Sneas' and 'Bunoscionn', each with their unique style of musical performance and all willing to do the gig for the love of music. What strikes me most is the amazing talent that exists among young people and the incredible passion that music elicits from them.

It takes me some time to stop and view the reel of projected images on the wall. I find it jarring to say the least as they are larger than usual images of him. I see him togged out posing with the team as they win a cup final. I see him waving from the back of the youth club group shot. I see him dancing around in a small group. My mind is mentally assessing and recounting the shots I have not seen before and making a note to ask for copies of those captured moments.

Gregg comes to stand beside me. Always a rock of support, he has a natural capacity to feel solid and comforting even in the midst of his own heartache. My brother, who devoted his life to an ecovillage development, building a sustainable community from the ground up, commissioned the help of his nephew over the summer months, in the construction of his house made from cobb. This was a highlight in Darragh's short life as he got his first taste of independence and learned that when he slept in and showed up late for the job he would be docked pay. 'Fair enough,' Darragh replied to Gregg, when he was informed of this. Ciara made her first big driving debut as she drove us all on 'the longest trip ever' as Darragh described it, having to avoid motorways and use only national roads to Gregg's as we dropped the worker off for his first few days' labour.

It feels surreal watching these stills fade out as another comes to the fore. It's as if it is a movie of someone else's life. What I am looking at should be still happening now. How can that young person no longer exist as he presents in those shots? Happy, playful, having fun! How can he not be still here? The evening draws to a close and my predominant feeling is of gratefulness for the family, friends and community that reached out, not only to me but into the wider community to support, aid and educate in the wake of such tragedy. Amazingly they raise exactly the price of the grave plot with €35 to spare, which is used to purchase a thank you bouquet for the main organiser, Josie.

The next morning dawns and neither Derek nor I slept well – me feeling so much anger and frustration, upset at the apparent injustice of my life. Another wave of the anger is such a contrast to the gratefulness I felt only hours before. Derek – holding space, holding me, helping me express and feel my way through the wave of grief. So many images of this day the previous year floods my consciousness: the search party, the tree, him frozen in time. I want them to stop but they won't and so they play through and I'm held in love and understanding as the ebb and flow of intense emotions flood my mind.

The car trip to Tara is filled with a myriad of emotional expressions as the roller coaster continues. A few cars are already gathered at the hill when we arrive, and we take off on foot, in no particular order, up to the hill itself where the expansive view helps give a wider perspective. It feels lighter up here and I'm struck by the feeling of history in the broader sense, along with my own. The ancient seat of the High Kings of Ireland.

The first time I ever saw my children with their dad and his partner was at a collective photoshoot taking place on the hill. An artist, Paul Geraghty, choreographed a living sculpture as a way to highlight and protest the re-routing of a motorway through this ancient site. Over 1,500 people showed up to form the words 'Save Tara Valley' and the outline of a harp, our national emblem, on Tara and an adjoining patch of field. This project, a massive undertaking to say the least, required months of planning and much logistical organising. The local papers had advertised a request for people to partake. Being without the children for the weekend as they visited their dad, Gregg and I decided to become involved.

I had no idea Dave and his partner would show up at the event. Seeing them in the distance I was overwhelmed by the look of family that presented to me and the reality check that our family unit as we knew it no longer existed. This of course was not news to me but seeing it was so different, making it so real. Ciara and Darragh ran excitedly to greet and hug me, telling me about the helicopter that would take a picture of everybody lying on the grass and how they were going to be part of the harp.

'Gregg and I are going to be one of the strings of the harp and we have to go lie on the grass over there,' I replied, trying to sound normal as I bit my lip. They laughed at the white suits we had been given to wear and urged us to try them on. After a few minutes, we were called to take our positions and they returned to Dave and his partner Sinead, a family friend they had known most of their lives. I was thankful they were assigned to a different part in the photo and so had to remain at the top of the hill while Gregg and I were sent way down to the other end of the field.

As I lay on the ground dressed in a white boiler suit with hundreds of others, a helicopter flying overhead taking the shot, the cool moist grass felt nurturing to my hot cheek. The green strands smelled of soil and I knew this living, growing plant life was without judgement as it swallowed my tears. No one but Gregg was aware what was transpiring for me. A moment of significance was unfolding for sure, for the country, as a political decision was challenged by an artist's vision, and personally, as my family was visibly altered. Excitedly the next day the kids and I tried to find ourselves in the photo in the newspaper.

Their dad and I met when I was barely twenty at a local rugby club dance. Tall and broad with a twinkle in his eye and a quick wit, Dave got my attention. Although I was very taken with him, I had spent most of my teenage years with one guy and was not ready for a relationship. Not long after that first encounter and a few dates I took off to the USA to work for a year. We rekindled our relationship shortly after my return and a year later we both then emigrated to California for three years where he worked as a landscape gardener in a climate that suited this work. I taught 4th–6th grade in a Montessori School. This was a period of great adventure, and life in the warm sun suited us both. We married in Ireland a few months after our return and settled back to the somewhat challenging feat of setting up a home and job hunting. For many years we lived happily, struggling at times with life, finances, climate change especially in his line of work, and a young daughter who began life with some medical struggles but who thankfully made a full recovery by the time she was three years old and just in time for the arrival of her brother. Children swallowed up our time and resources and while a few cracks showed from time to time, we carried on.

Eventually our lives began drifting apart on different paths – me, searching for some deeper meaning to it all. We did what we could to address some underlying problems until finally, two years after we had moved to a lovely new house in a country town and almost fifteen years married, we conceded that our marriage was beyond saving. It was a stressful few years that followed. For me that loss was immense, even though I knew it had to be. We did our best to stay amicable for the sake of our children, caught in the whirlwind of their secure world falling apart. Much effort was made to reassure them that they were loved, which kept both of us very present in their lives, and we hoped this would spare them some suffering. Not our finest hours as emotions flew high even with the best of arrangements but we did manage to sell our home and each of us moved on. We kept things light between us around the children and our contact was without bitterness or stress for the most part. And so Ciara and Darragh would spend every other weekend with him and Sinead.

Back on Tara, nine years later, on a cold December day, a random mix of friends and family have come to share Darragh's remembering day. We wander down into a wooded area and find rope swings. We play – pushing and pulling each other in these ready-made playground activities. The mood is light and fun; I can partake and be there having come out of the intensity of earlier. I know he would approve of the fun and frivolity; it was his way.

The warm, welcoming smell of home cooking envelopes us as we arrive into a nearby café. I have booked a table for our group which proves prudent as the place is alive with conversation and people seated at wooden tables. A nourishing lunch in the hillside café, most of us ordering soups and stews to warm us from the inside out, is the perfect antidote to our extended time in the cold air. The food tastes exquisite as it seems to melt in my mouth before heating me. After our coffees and chat, we make our way to the infamous well. This is more challenging and a solemnity descends naturally over the group. We settle around the well, protected by the infamous gate, seated on grass verges and stone walls, and the story of Darragh's adventure with the revered water, as told at the funeral, is now recounted by Gregg along with other anecdotes from his time with us. This day of acknowledging Darragh and his passing feels appropriate and fitting. I'm almost disappointed he hasn't made his presence known to one or all of us in some way. However, my desperation for connection with him often prohibits me experiencing anything at all. The day runs its course and comes to a natural parting of the group. Ciara returns to Kevin's and I realise I cannot face home this night and choose to stay in Derek's where sleep is more likely. There isn't much breathing space as the hurdle of Christmas approaches.

Chapter 14
Christmas tree

Great gnarly branches spread out over my head as the solid bark feels like a spine behind me. Exposed — the leaves no longer give cover to shield the raw vulnerable condition in which I have arrived here. Nonetheless this familiar beech tree is my saviour in this moment. Lost in my own pain, I've been driving for nearly an hour. It's Christmas Day and I'm trying to get to my parents' home where my family will be meeting to go through the motions of Christmas.

It is customary in our family for us to spend Christmas Day together, and for many years this happened in our home as I have children and my siblings don't. As I near my parents' house I divert and turn around to the road to our home where he, his sister and I shared our lives and which, in ordinary circumstances, would have been the venue for this day. I pull in, realising my distress makes me dangerous on the road. Where to go? Where to be? It's as if I cannot escape myself and this desperation. Derek is having Christmas breakfast with his ex-wife and daughter. That does not feel like the place to be either! I feel totally out of control, not sure what to do next. Then an image of the beech tree comes to me — the infamous tree where the kiss that wasn't a kiss transpired. I know it's a place I will find solace. And so I pull myself together enough to drive there.

As I walk through the park and greet some early morning walkers and kids trying out shiny new bikes, I can barely lift my gaze to meet any of it. Finally, the tree, and I fall at the foot of this king of nature and dissolve until the sobs subside and I can get to my feet and stand resting against its solid bark, letting it hold me. In this moment nothing matters except my breathing – the sky blue, the air sharp as my lungs inhale, the majesty of the big blue fir tree opposite. Who cares what day it is, or what the world is doing right now? I am fighting to hold on to some semblance of sanity and composure. I have no idea how long I stay here holding on for dear life, as waves of fear are now added to the distress that my body may not be able to function as required in the face of this level of feeling. And so I stay there waiting, repeating the words, 'I am OK and safe and there is no need for drama.'

I recall the last time my legs felt as if they couldn't hold me. It was in the first weeks after Darragh's passing and I went to stay with Derek in a hotel for a night. I thought the new surroundings would bring some distraction if not comfort. The city was twinkling with Christmas festivities and lights as we arrived. A large, beautifully decorated tree filled the window where I sat, leaving enough space to see the street. I watched a youth walk unsteadily, as if on drugs, across traffic. His clothing was too flimsy for the weather and I felt a fleeting moment of gratitude – Darragh was safe from the cold, at least. I was not lying awake, night after night, wondering where he was, as mothers of sons and daughters who get mixed up in the drug world do.

Derek was meeting some people from dance class for a Christmas celebration, and I had assured him I was fine to be left alone. In fact, I liked the anonymity of the hotel and yet Christmas was like a planet I had no understanding of. I watched the throngs of people walk along busy streets, laden with bags, each rushing to fulfil some wish list of their beloved. I wondered if we were all mad or if I was just living an altered state of reality. Up until then, I had enjoyed a healthy attitude to the festivities or so I thought. I liked the excuse for pause and time with friends and family, despite the extra financial pressure it always seems to create, no matter how carefully it was planned. But the commerciality of it, that particular time, seemed so brash and unspirited. I felt like an alien.

A night of the most intense feeling transpired for me. Derek left me with a warm scented bath and all was fine until reality hit, really hard – Darragh was dead; he wasn't coming back. I called Derek, as we had arranged if the need arose. The need arose. I couldn't contain the enormity of loss and intense sadness that flooded me. I was raw and torn asunder. It was early days and I had yet to ascertain the best way through the onslaught.

The following day, two old friends of mine, Chris and Debbie, offered to pick me up from Derek's and drive me home. During that time, I was rarely alone; I wasn't yet trusted to drive myself anywhere as people kept a watchful eye on me. This couple I met when we were teenagers as they were friends of my first love. They remained a couple and kept in touch. Our families frequented Sunday picnics and walks together in forests and beaches as their two sons and our son and daughter grew up. We shared our parenting stories and experiences. Our children, having no cousins of similar age, regarded them as family.

At the front door of my home, my legs gave way as I tried to turn the key in the door and walk in to the space where Darragh had been laid out only two weeks before. Debbie, standing beside me, totally panicked and shouted to her husband, 'Come here quick and hug her or something.' We have shared a laugh since about that moment as she recounts her reaction and the first thing that came to her mind. In the face of adversity, it's good to smile.

Here I am a year later, in this place of pain, trying to carry out a now meaningless tradition of celebrating Christmas. My phone summons me back to now and I feel a responsibility to answer. I have been off the airwaves for a time, and it has been ringing as family and partner are looking for me. 'There's no need for drama,' I repeat to myself, 'we have all had enough,' and so I answer this time. It happens to be Gregg. However, words won't come easily as I try and explain that I am OK and tell him where I am.

As an earthy man, connected very much to nature, he understands completely that this would be a place to find some strength. He also knows it is quite near Derek's and he insists I get that far. I concede. It makes sense; I am not really fit to drive any distance. And so begins what feels like a pilgrimage to the car park. One foot in front of the other; never before have I understood mindfulness as I do in this slow, shaky, unsteady walk. One wobbly step and then another – 'Inhale, exhale,' I say to myself as I snail along the path, oblivious now to other walkers. How can happy smiling shiny faces, filled with the excitement of Santa's deliveries, coexist in the park with me in this shell of existence? I barely remember the short drive and as my partner opens the door to me, he enfolds me and asks his ex-wife and daughter to do the same to give me strength. Meanwhile, Louise is on route to get me. No driving for me today. So much for my mantra of 'there's no need for drama'! So begins the second Christmas Day without him.

In my parents' home, we all have our moments. Ciara, normally inclined to be less emotionally expressive than me, her mother, falls apart when I present a locket to her with his and her photo inside. It was a thought that popped into my head one day and whilst looking for the right one I met Sharon, who had been instrumental in creating the magic cocoon in our local community centre for Darragh's funeral ceremony. She was accompanied by her teenage daughter, Leah, who is the same age and was friendly with Darragh. They helped me choose the most appropriate locket. Whilst the shop was engraving it, we went to have coffee. Upon our return, we were astounded by the sound of 'Don't you worry, don't you worry child, heaven has a plan for you,' resonating from the shop speakers. Leah turned to embrace me with tears in her eyes as she knew he had come to me in a dream singing those words. It was the most perfect gift for Ciara, and we both knew it in that moment. Then the shop owner realised her teenage daughter also knew Darragh and gave me a discount. I became teary then, knowing he was there supporting me in this. To top it all, that day finished with a call from Louise, saying she had deposited funds into my account to help with bills outstanding and Christmas. What an amazing family I have.

Christmas dinner is interspersed with fun accounts of my family's adventures in the world. My youngest brother Ken, who is working in the music business, had recently returned from Los Angeles where his main man of the moment was recording an album. We are fascinated by our youngest sibling's rock and roll life and his witty commentary. Ken regularly infuses light and fun into conversations with his sharp wit and affable personality, something that has been part of him since his youth. These light moments are coupled with poignant, 'hard to swallow your food' moments, as Darragh, in his absence, makes himself known. Thankfully, it's a far cry from my morning experience. We raise our glasses in toast to honour him and the love we shared with him. His grandparents, possibly less equipped than their offspring in processing such levels of grief, seem to be manifesting feelings of helplessness around me. My mother, producing a dinner fit for kings, is watchful as she observes how little I can eat. Their eldest child is so broken and they cannot help to mend or fix me; a natural parental need.

I know this place. I feel it with Ciara and I am grateful every moment I witness her stoically live with this gaping wound. She stays in college and manages to sit exams and do assignments. I feel such pride tinged with sadness. Always a responsible sort, she has had to grow up overnight and live with something many never have to experience. Her boyfriend Kevin and his family provide her with a safe place to be and whilst I often wish for her to live at home, I understand her choice. It is that natural stage of life, time to leave the nest, but this feels sudden, his departure acting as a catalyst, catapulting her into a decision that may have naturally unfolded at a more incremental rate. Again, I count my blessings that they are there to provide her with that support she cannot get with me. I am a prominent part of the wound and pain and around each other we try and hold back to protect each other. It's not even a conscious decision; it's natural parent–child conditioning.

As the day unfolds we exchange gifts, our little forever-altered family, and while I am so grateful for the love and support of my family around me, each of them feeling their loss in their own way,

I also want to get out of there. It's like I cannot play the charade of trying to continue with normal Christmas. Darragh would have been sitting up late with the adults and partaking in whatever games ensued – Trivial Pursuit, flicking coins with my brothers and father, cards and darts which came to be in the latter years. He enjoyed the witty comments, the playful competition and fun my family engaged in and would have been reluctant to retire to bed.

I return to Derek's that evening and a flood of relief fills me. I didn't even know I was holding my breath in the face of my family. I didn't know I was holding it all together in their company until I left them. There is no manual on how to be, how to live, how to carry on when left bereft by the sudden death of the youngest member of your family unit. I am grateful for the loving arms of Derek that night and the feeling I can be anything I need to be, an emotional wreck, a crying mess, a loving partner. It's all OK here with him. Here I can let down all walls. It's worth its weight in gold.

Chapter 15
The bridge

With Christmas out of the way, a sense of relief ensues. My special leave comes into effect and work is not asking anything of me. A year has passed since he left, and it feels like five minutes on the one hand and forever on the other. The big trip to Thailand is scheduled for February after the fundraising event, and I'm a bit all over the place. It is, I concede, a pretty amazing opportunity. Who gets to down tools and head away to an exotic island in Thailand for six weeks on the strength of a cohort of family and friends who are happy to have a knees-up into the bargain? Who gets to wake up to the reality of the dramatic turn of events that faces me, day in and day out?

New Year's Eve dawns and not being one for too much hype, a quiet night in with Derek is on the cards. Before I leave for his house, a contingent of the crew call in with cards and a Christmas present for me and Ciara. I am touched by their thoughtfulness. They address one to Ciara as a thank you to her for all the years of being their babysitter. Fighting over TV rights and driving them places when no one else would, more like, but she is delighted with their sentiment. I waver on the brink of tears and without pause for further sentiment they begin to recount stories of their Christmas exploits which she and I enjoy.

The eldest of the crew, now turned seventeen, describes being asked to go out to help his dad in their garden only to find him dressed as Santa, white beard and all, sitting in a car, which is an older model in need of a little tweaking (the car not his dad of course), but a car nonetheless. What a lovely gesture by this family; the joy and pain the story evokes simultaneously is hard to contain. A responsible guy, he works hard during school breaks to make his contribution to the household and this present is a just reward. Polished and shined up, this is now a prize for him and a reflection of how these lads are getting older and life is moving on.

He offers to take us on a test run. 'I'm not ready to drive the lads around yet, but I can make an exception for you two,' he says, ignoring the promises of the lads to behave in the car. And so we go on a little tour of our little town, passengers in the eldest of the crew's car. It hardly seems real. How can time have moved so fast? How much growing can happen in a year? 'Forever Fifteen', that's our place in time. I find this reality frustrating beyond comprehension – my member of this particular crew forever frozen in time. All stories, reminiscences of days gone by.

Upon our return to our home, a couple of the girls of the original crew have arrived also. They have become a little less frequent in their visits but tend to speak of Darragh more fluidly when they come. One of the lads offers to make tea for all present for 'old time's sake'. Naturally I am happy to oblige. They urge me to sit down and open my gift and card. A little apprehensively, I concede, because emotions are close to the surface. I unwrap the jagged edges of the taped paper to reveal two packets of Darragh's favourite chocolate bars; their orange and blue wrappers threaten to open the water floodgates. These bars are a favourite and so regularly consumed by all present. The banter flies as they apologise as to the short life of the gift. 'We will be eating those now of course,' they laugh, as, true to form, they begin consuming the said chocolate. Again I laugh through tears as I am endeared by them and this feels like a more usual way of being within these four walls.

This is the life I know! I am a parent with one young adult daughter and a son in his teens. I am supposed to be wondering how a twelve-pack of taxi bars can have disappeared so quickly. I am supposed to be fretting about the new car and what that means and setting boundaries for how this New Year's Eve is spent. Instead, I am drinking tea with his friends, eating his favourite bars and wondering what went wrong. We laugh as they remember the June thunderstorm when the town got flooded and they came for shelter in this house, making a movie of the weather as narrated by the proud new car owner. One of them was dancing out in the deluge of rain, soaked to the skin for the special impact and to demonstrate the effects of the level of rain, unheard of in this town especially in June. Darragh ran back to save and rescue the damsel in distress and the lads cheered and clapped to camera as Darragh and said young woman ran for cover to the front door. We ask to look at the movie, still recorded on one of their phones. It is a hilarious, happy account of a day in the life of a group of teenagers. Enthusiasm for life is the predominant feeling leaping out of the images of all involved, with no clues there as to what was coming down the tracks.

After they leave and Ciara leaves for Kevin's, the house again feels so much more empty than before, as if it swells with the activity and life and then contracts and shrinks back to the shell that it is now. Suddenly I am glad I am not to spend the evening here. I speak to his photo as I often do, 'I miss that life. I ache inside to hear your voice. I miss everything about you even the annoying bits. I miss the lads, the constant opening and shutting of the front door, the kitchen cupboard doors and the noisy interruptions of my daily existence with queries and questions and debates on ordinary things. The need for a lift to football, to the next town, to the cinema. The feeling of chaos as you and the crew swept through the house and out again just as quick, or spill out of the car, crammed with bodies as we drive to Newbridge, music blasting and the car vibrating in response. Help me and Ciara and the lads to get through this, day by day, hour by hour, moment by moment, in this coming year.'

I especially remind him to keep an eye on his crew as they navigate this loss in a society that uses alcohol to sidestep dealing with feelings especially amongst that age group and most particularly with males. They have in moments expressed feelings of sadness, frustration and even rage at the insanity of his act and the effect on all of them left behind. Sometimes on a visit to me, especially in smaller groups of two or three, there is more freedom to express. His joined-at-the-hip friend stomps around the sitting room raging and furious at Darragh for leaving them. 'For fuck sake Darragh, why didn't you talk to me?' he exclaims in tears of exasperation.

Another sits quietly. 'I am just sad, I am so sad,' he sobs as tears are spilling down his face. Usually known for his mime act of a country and western number, which is witty and entertaining, this is a difficult contrast to witness. Some of the girls would come occasionally to talk of how they missed him and how they don't quite know what to do with their feelings. One of the girls talks of the fear amongst parents that they might follow suit. 'I feel like I can't go to my room to cry without someone checking to see if I am harming myself,' she says, 'and it's so frustrating. I am sad, I miss him, I want to scream at the sky but I am afraid they will send me to the nut house.'

The school has set up a programme of support as has the local youth club and I remind the teens of these services. In some instances they tell me that they don't find them useful. Are some of these teens holding back their true level of feelings? I encourage them to be real with their feelings and not hold back as I feel it may help, but I am aware they may need other supports. And of course their presence has that paradoxical effect again of pain and pleasure rolled in to each moment we share. I note lately that their talk of feelings seems now to be associated with stories of nights out and drink taken rather than in the cold light of day in my company.

What is my role I wonder? Is there a place for me to support them? I know this crew will maybe grow apart from each other and I will see so much less of them as is the ever-changing nature of life. However, the bond of this experience will connect all of us for many years to come, of that I have no doubt. Each of them holds a special place in my heart. The arrival of the car into their lives; one of them driving; the end of the school cycle for some and only one year left for others – all indicative of time moving and things changing.

And so the new year begins, and in no time the support team are setting dates for revamping my home so that I can rent it out upon my return from the great adventure, and the banks can be appeased when payments can be met. In the meantime, I find myself really stuck. I sit in my bedroom and look absentmindedly through boxes and bags that got moved up to this space over the funeral days. Ashamedly, I realise they have been there for more than a year and I have had no enthusiasm or interest in reallocating their original space to them.

I leaf through paperwork and am surprised by an occasional gem in the form of an unseen photo or a birthday card. I am grateful the house is not being let out to new people before I go, as I realise that would be an incredibly big leap to take. I can barely sort out this minor mess and yet the revampers, with paint and polish, are pushing me to get sorting just by their enthusiasm. His bedroom remains a place of comfort for me and so I go there to lie on his bed, just to feel closer to him. My life has taken off in a new direction suddenly. It is bringing me to the other side of the world. How much can change in a short period of time.

Chapter 16
Home revamp

The doorbell rings and I'm greeted by a team of cheery, smiling faces in yellow vests, painting clothes and even a hard hat for fun. This team of volunteers evolved from the '*meetings about me*', and have come to put my house in order so that when I return I can consider moving out. I welcome them with trepidation. Already the preparation for their arrival has a profound effect as I move and rearrange and clear space for fresh paint to spill over the walls. Derek once again is holding me in the raw space I occupy awaiting the imminent arrival. A new coat of paint, a clean covering for the sad walls! I wonder if I can cover up the quivering I feel inside.

Much ado about the leader and who is in charge of this operation combines the sense of adventure and fun with the practical task at hand. James, a sweet man, both by profession and nature, a long-time friend and one of the most generous and giving people you could meet, is getting a hard time for his self-professed lack of ability to draw a straight line not to mind paint.

Ladders, paint tins, drills, bits and masking tape all arrive in plastic boxes as each person brings a useful collection of tools. An ambitious plan to repaint most of the house, save his room and mine, is the object for the weekend. And so it begins: loud music, sanding, staining and painting. Smells choke the air as paint colours the walls, lifting the shades to a notable vibrancy. Combined skills, friends and family once again united in supporting me. There's quiet chatter in some rooms as the assembled crew prep and paint. A loud uproar of laughter upstairs as an ingenious plan to reach the unreachable high point unfolds in what sounds like a comedic episode on a television screen. The arranging and logistics bring to the fore that primal male coding that likes to solve and fix a problem. A very precarious balancing act worthy of a circus ring ensues and the uppermost point is duly painted and is met with a collective sigh of relief. No one comes out the worse for wear despite the inherent danger.

The large pots of soup and stew that I made the evening before provide some sustenance as the working party fill the kitchen space for lunch. A random visit from a few of 'his crew', as they stop in upon the intensely alive activity-filled space, evokes memories of happy days in the house, once a regular pit stop for them. They smile and laugh and join in the banter and graciously avoid getting a paint brush in hand but stay a while joking with the workers over missed bits, stripped paint and wondering if there are any biscuits and tea going? Should you arrive upon the scene you'd be forgiven for thinking that a celebration of life was taking place! In some ways maybe that is the case. The human capacity to row in and collectively support in creative and ingenious ways certainly comes to be in this instance. In the face of adversity, human friendships shine forth in a way that was previously unimagined.

Break over, back to work, everyone returns to their particular activity including me, when out of nowhere, it comes like a derailed train – the devastation under this wondrous scene floods me. I'm looking for somewhere to be away from the working team. My home is invaded, there's nowhere to go. I retreat into the shower, sit on a stool, paint scraper in hand, in the waterless space save for the floods of tears that flow from me. I cannot contain the sobs as the lull of chat and laughter fades into the background. Why now with all this happening? I'm frustrated at the enormity of emotion that spills over and renders me useless. I'm found out. Paula discovers me. The sunny nurturer of my inner circle gently closes the door behind her, acknowledging that I'm best left alone. Minutes later, a scout comes to check in. I just need to be left here; in this place that is the most desolate, lonely place in the world! None of those amazing people could know this feeling.

I stay there in my shower until the waves of tears and sobs abate as I know they will. Time passes and I recover enough to re-enter the space. I gingerly interact, fragile to the core, and for the most part the painters carry on regardless. I feel their sense of not knowing what to do around me and I am glad they leave me to my own devices.

It's getting late – time to down tools and regroup the following day. I'm thankful for the return of the less crowed space, and wearily and gratefully I fall into bed, allowing myself to be held in love by Derek. The next morning begins with a similar start. Fresh-faced, smiling friends and family arrive suitably attired, in dribs and drabs, ready to continue the mission: painting with rollers, cutting in with brushes; steady hands a requirement for the latter. Sharon's arrival with a cooked chicken creates an outburst of hilarious, entertaining and witty comments as an official lunch break takes precedence over the work.

Progress is quick with so many hands on deck, transforming the place into a fresh paint-smelling lightened space. Furniture is rearranged and things look so new. I can almost feel him smiling now from his place over the fire on the newly tinted wall, as Ciara and I sit with him chatting about the incredible weekend that just transpired.

Chapter 17
Trip to Thailand

The twelve-hour flight turns out not to be as bad as I had anticipated. I share four seats with a woman who has as little interest in speaking to me as I do to her. We have a mutual understanding that the seat space is shared and if we are careful we can both lie down and get some shut eye. There is something almost freeing about being up in the sky in a timeless zone with nothing to do but be on the journey. I feel quite happy and almost excited at the madness of me sitting so far above the earth, crossing time zones to a place further than I have ever been before. The attire of the Malaysian airline staff is so Eastern looking I feel like I am going really far away, which is a fact. All those wonderful people whom I love and love me are left at home doing their thing. And now, I am far away above the clouds like he is.

I imagine Darragh on the wing or surfing on top of the plane as we travel. Somehow it feels good to imagine such things. Can he bring us, his family, his crew, his friends to mind at will? Does he have a mind operating anymore? Does he know I am making this great trip, going on this great adventure?

I am interrupted by the smiling air hostess asking if I would like earphones. I am fascinated by the high-tech screen in front of me. I can watch movies, TV, box sets or play music. It has something for everyone, of all ages and cultures. All of this on the back of the seat in front of me. I find myself half interested in a movie for a time and time passes quickly enough inbetween random walks up and down the plane, food breaks, writing in my ever-present journal, observing my co-passengers from a distance, trying to block out the snoring of co-travellers, indulging in short snoozes and trips to the suction flushing toilets. They never cease to startle me with the sudden and loud sound each time I press the button and the very blue water swirls in and disappears as fast.

I disembark in Kuala Lumpur and find myself extremely grateful my rucksack is carrying on, without my intervention, to the next destination. A couple of hours hanging around the airport don't give me much of a feeling for the Malaysian city, but I do feel a sense of adventure. I barely recollect the next flight, as exhaustion takes hold and I cannot keep myself awake for any level of awareness. Suddenly it's time to get off the plane, collect my luggage and find the ferry. The sense of adventure quickly fades to weary traveller as my brother's rucksack weighs heavily on my back, undisputedly heavier than I remember at the point of departure.

As I arrive outside to the postcard-like scene of the airport in Ko Samui – the structure of wooden poles framed by the roof of grass – the heat slams me and I feel both terror and excitement. Everything looks so different, reminding me I have arrived somewhere else in the world, miles away from my Western experience and life to date. The air feels heavy and almost moist with the heat that saturates the air, and the faint smell of sewage hangs around my nostrils as if trapped by the heavy droplets. I take the taxi van to the pier where a light sea breeze clears the smell and fans my hot skin. While waiting, I spend the time observing the predominantly young, long-legged, tanned backpackers accompanying me on the pier as, in the distance, the ferry docks at the flimsy wooden bridge. We walk out to meet it on the most precarious looking wooden structure, rickety poles held together with a binding of sorts. The walk is made ever more challenging by my rucksack which I find is tipping me backwards. The poles, not planed, are stick-like in appearance and uneven under foot. A gangplank slopes downwards from the bridge to the ferry deck and as I await my turn to step on, I inwardly gasp at the perilousness of the next step I am about to take. Wobbly and uncertain of foot, I walk down the sloped plank and land on the deck. The deck is spattered with long browned legs, some hairy and some smooth, escaping from under shorts or dresses; everyone is wearing flip-flops. Backpacks, suitcases and yoga mats are stacked in the middle of the floor space. People fill every seat and as there are none left, I find myself sitting on my oversized bag as we wait to leave the pier.

Despite my total exhaustion rendering an almost out of body feeling, the incredible sights do impact on me – the blue-green water as it swishes against the boat, the masses of lush greenery that covers the mountains framing the landscape in the tropical jungle, the beautiful sea breeze warmly caressing this tired, pretty old, crumpled body, worn out from a day and a half of travelling nonstop. Time is immaterial, body clock totally confused, I am barely awake to the journey that lands me on yet another rickety bridge. I walk, unsteady and over burdened by my travel kit, this time to a beach. Locals with signboards stand touting for business amongst the fresh dispatch of tourists, eager to carry us to the array of beach communities that are dotted along the coastline. I stand next to a sign for my desired destination. A small group of four of us assemble at this particular place, and I find myself needing to stand in some shade. An Irish accent feels like a gift in the midst of my unfamiliar, now extremely hot and decidedly uncomfortable surroundings. I need to get cool and lie down and lose the luggage and it is all feeling a bit much.

We quickly establish that we four are going to the same place and we are all just arriving from various European and Indian destinations. Daithí, the Irish traveller, has just left India and is familiar with this part of the locality. He was here last year. The boatman comes to discuss a price and is pretty determined to charge us a lot more than is usual. I leave the negotiations to my fellow countryman who is just as clear he won't pay over the odds for the trip. They eventually find a middle ground to which we are all agreeable and it's time to get on board the next boat. This time, it is a smaller vessel, much like a rowing boat with an adapted engine, a very long pole and propeller at the back. The job of clambering over the side into the boat that bobs up and down on the shoreline proves to be rather taxing for me. I'm close to tears as I try to manoeuvre myself and baggage over the side of the boat. A kind young Dutch guy offers to take my rucksack, and I am so grateful.

And so the four of us now find ourselves sitting in the longboat as the boatman touts for more passengers to join our little entourage. After what seems like an age, as I feel myself frying in the direct sun, he returns none the happier as he has been unsuccessful and we take off. The speed of the boat as it courses through the choppy water beneath the jungle-clad mountain is exhilarating to say the least. I love the proximity of the water as it sprays the salty mist onto my overheated body. I sit behind a Swedish girl and her hair blows in the wind, exposing the side of her tanned young face to me as we speed through the water. All too quickly it is time to disembark around the bay at the next beach. Again, I find my climb out of the boat and into the shallow water both undignified and challenging. The Dutch angel has my rucksack in hand already and the four of us are left on this magical beach in the heat of the midday sun.

All around us scantily clad sun-worshippers sit and chat in shady spots beneath the coconut trees. I see hammocks beckoning me to come and sit in them. The magic soon fades as we find there is no room in this particular establishment. The island is particularly busy and they operate on a first come, first served basis. No bookings. The guy behind the desk explains that there is currently an accommodation crisis on the island. This is not music to my ears as I ask for his recommendation. I try to contact my friend who lives there but discover she is in Malaysia on a visa run for a few days. Daithí knows the lie of the land and suggests we head in the direction of what he considers to be our best option. I am incredulous as he points across to a sheer incline rising up from the beach over the cliff face. The first step is unfeasibly steep. My one bag feels like lead on my back and I know that without the Dutch guy, Art, offering to carry my rucksack, I would not have made it.

It's like a pilgrimage to the next hostelry. We pick our way carefully along the root-riddled jungle trail, high up on the cliff, but I am so consumed with getting one foot in front of the other I cannot take in the spectacular views. We begin to descend again across a long, wooden pole bridge, much resembling the one at the pier. It is barely attached to the cliff face. We go down more stone steps, carved in a non-uniform way out of the cliff face. The terrain is tricky and calls for full alertness as we traipse in single file. We arrive at the next hostelry to the same story. Two more places later and after another ascent and descent in the hot sun, I am frazzled and hot and hardly able to speak. The other three, notwithstanding having youth on their side and being seasoned travellers, are also beginning to show signs of frayed edges. Art is sweating profusely and his T-shirt is stuck to him. I am in awe of his strength carrying both our bags. 'You will have to buy me a new shirt,' he says as we pause to catch our breath. Charlotte, the young and beautiful Swedish girl, is beginning to crack as she sighs heavily, exclaiming, 'I cannot go much further.' She has carried a sizeable load across this hostile terrain. We set off again to the last outpost which has literally nothing beyond it but sheer cliff and dense jungle.

They say they have two beds in a shared room, and we can go and look. Charlotte goes first as I try to gather myself and comes back looking a little forlorn and despondent. I follow and within moments dissolve into quiet tears. Six narrow bunks fill up the tiny space. Four are already inhabited by an array of bags, and people squeezed into the very small space with only a top bunk left that is right beside the toilet door. As I nudge open the door to expose the squatty toilet, a hole in the ground with a grey-looking tiled surround, it's enough to push me over the edge. After all that travelling over the past two days I just could not envisage staying here. I close my eyes and very determinedly speak to Darragh in my mind: 'I am not sleeping in a top bunk. I am not you. I am not a teenager. I am too old and tired for this shit. You better do something from where you are and find me a decent bed.' Suddenly I feel every year of my forty-eight years weighing down on me as I walk dejectedly back to the others.

What kind of madness is this? Here I am on the other side of the world, no one I know, not to mind love, around me. The heat, the exhaustion, the travel, the unfamiliar surroundings – I am feeling scared and really old.

Meanwhile, the others have had time to regroup and get rehydrated and have come up with a plan. On the other side, back where we first landed, deeper into the jungle, there are a couple more places. The men would go back and the women could mind the luggage and even have something to eat while they went. Something very primal exists in this arrangement.

I very clearly state that no matter what the cost I would prefer a bed to myself and failing that, I would share with Charlotte. The men nod in an understanding way and set off back across the challenging terrain. I get to know a little more about Charlotte. She is in her early twenties and, finding herself between jobs, has taken some time out. She has been on the road for some months now, loves the adventure and has already explored Vietnam and Laos.

'That was a tough journey today,' she says, wiping perspiration from her brow, 'those hills are very steep'. That she is finding today's challenge more stressful than usual somewhat comforts me. Travelling doesn't necessarily need to be so difficult. We keep our conversation general enough and wonder how successful the runners are. Neither of us relishes the idea that we may have to take the bunks in the already crowded room.

I now get to look around at where I am. I am astounded by the beauty of the place. We are perched at the side of a mountain on a wooden platform extending out above ocean waves lapping up against the rocks beneath us. Views of the bay, as it curves around to the beach we just traversed, are breathtaking. Mountains with lush greenery, like spines on a hedgehog, are expansive, reaching up towards the clear, deep blue sky. It is a spectacle to behold. I make a mental note to revisit this place when I am settled in accommodation.

The men return with good news. Art has put a deposit on a bungalow for me. They will hold it for an hour. I barely know this man and he has taken responsibility for my well-being. We joke about his good fortune in sharing a boat with me. All four of us in fact have a bed for the night. Art carries my load again, one more time, back across the terrain. 'You are in debt of two T-shirts to me now. I have been sweating so much they will never be clean again,' he jokes as we part company. The four of us now part ways after our bonding experience of the accommodation crisis and our initiation to this place. Each retreats to their own space, out of the sun — a space to lay down and get some rest.

An hour later, I'm lying in a hammock on my deck outside my bungalow coming to terms with this new environment. The interesting toilet arrangement of a hose and water bucket is one which I have not yet fully figured out. I am grateful, however, that the toilet is not just a hole in the ground. The big net hanging over the bed, the raised floor in the musty wooden cabin, is calling to me to question what roams beneath. All of which is so much better than that top bunk. I even have shelves and this wooden deck with a hammock. It is, I note, rather dirty around my cabin and I tend not to care in this moment. I can rest. I nod off in the shaded hammock to be woken suddenly by a cat with sharp claws clawing up under the hammock. It's sore as it scratches my cloth-shaped outline. I grumpily declare to him, 'I am sorry if this is your space, cat, but I am here now, so go away.' He persists in poking at me with sharp claws.

I hastily clamber out of the hammock, tipping myself over and spilling on to the ground. In a very petulant way, I close the door of the cabin, vowing not to come out again until I can reschedule a trip home. This, for sure, is a disaster. Recover from Darragh's suicide? This place would certainly not be conducive to recovery. I cannot find any solace or peace here. How foolish am I? I am no backpacker; I cannot even carry my own bag for more than five minutes. Why am I not at home making plans with my partner, daughter and friends? I don't belong here.

Chapter 18
Thailand at the water's edge

The sound of a gecko calling startles me to wakefulness. In the darkness, I take a moment to stabilise my now incredibly fast heartbeat and remember where I am. Interestingly, I fall back to sleep. Does sleep come easier here because of the heat, the sound of the waves, or because of the clean air of the oversized jungle greenery? Whatever the attributing factors, I am grateful for better-quality slumber.

Settling in to this new space and pace of life has been made easier by the magnificence of the terrain around me. I live on what I call 'Main Street', in a row of cabins. Each contains a bedroom, a loo and a sink. A cold shower is as far as comforts go. Little cabins dot the hill behind me way up upon the rocks. Jungle abounds and trees are laden with fruits and coconut palms. Rocks and boulders provide the backdrop and cover for creatures and wildness I don't like to think about too much.

As the days unfold into weeks, a strange kind of familiar feeling begins to emerge – one of self-contentment and ease; a feeling that reminds me of me before I became a responsible adult with children and mortgages. Barely tangible and fleeting at first but perceptible and without need for me to try or do anything to foster it, it's coming of its own accord. My body starts to unravel and exhaustion dominates, to the point where some days, I feel like I haven't got the energy to digest food, and so my body calls me to detox naturally. Juices and coconut becomes the order of the dietary day as simply any other food is rejected by my body. This lasts for ten days. Strangely it causes me to smile, as I have avoided detoxes with great fervour in the past, and here my body has given me no choice.

The options for eating are surprisingly European in nature. Each cluster of huts has a restaurant attached and by way of duty, you are expected to eat at least one meal a day in the particular café or restaurant that you rent a hut from. This I learned the hard way when I was summoned to reception and told in no uncertain terms I would not be welcome to continue renting from them unless I ate meals there. I was totally flabbergasted at this demand but conceded and got my body back to eating, as this place suited my needs far more than that first night's accommodation.

The fact that there is nothing pressing, nothing that has to get done any day, allows me the freedom to follow my inner guidance. It is such a novel experience having no one to look after, no one's needs to be met and no meals to prepare. Laundry is even taken care of by your hosting cabin group for a small fee. The wonders of living in such remoteness provide endless entertainment – watching the activity as the boats come and go, navigated by the long poles through the mostly calm blue-green waters, bringing new arrivals with backpacks and yoga mats to our side of the island.

These boats are the lifeline of this part of the island, bringing food supplies, bottled water and even gas and oil. The only other access is across the mountain which is a jungle without even a proper road, so a large, four-wheeled pickup truck is about all that can cross this path. The thrill of this drive surpasses any roller coaster, as the jeep throws its passengers forward and back as it navigates the hills. A few brave walkers make it across with a Swiss jungle trekker called Yahtri, known for his knowledge of the path, who leads a party a couple of times a week. I have realised my limitations and have declined his invites. He and I become good friends; we are of a similar age and have great discussions on beliefs, life and nature. He, having lived in an ashram for a time in India, has incredible tales of his experiences and has taken to the jungle as if made for the wild terrain. 'I don't know how I ended up being born in Switzerland,' he quips, 'I was made for heat and jungle.'

There is time for that here. Time to stop, sit and talk with someone. Time to get to know what their life has shown them to date and learn how they ended up here, on this remote piece of the world. Time to sit on a cushion on the floor in a windowless café sipping a fruit shake watching the waves crash against the rocks or the dogs as they square up on either end of the beach for their daily territorial dance. This pace of life is wonderful in its ease.

One of my spiritual teachers, Don Hanson, is here from the States doing a couple of workshops over ten days and the timing is great. Don really supports me in allowing, observing and trusting that my body and spirit are helping me to unwind the trauma, the devastation and shock out of my system. He helps me follow my inner guidance and trust this part of me. These workshops create the opportunity to form lovely friendships and deep connections with people that feel real without knowing much of their day-to-day lives. We meet each day and sit in meditation to open up the life force in us and express and clear anything that holds us back from our true nature; that being joy and love.

At one such workshop the emotional devastation flows out of me; I fear it will never stop. The underlying feeling is as if life spat me out and gave the two fingers to all that I have worked towards on a personal level. The cruelty of such a twist of fate is difficult, especially as I have chosen to live consciously for many years. What does that even mean? It means I've been taking responsibility for my thinking and examining my conditioned beliefs. It means I have looked under the rocks of my past to see where I have held myself back, felt undeserving, not good enough or blamed others for my feeling bad. I lived a life where I looked for love and learning in all experiences and remained non-judgemental of myself and others as much as I could. It means I have been living a life which didn't just follow the herd, a life which has asked the difficult questions, a life where I sometimes made difficult choices, all the while following that same inner guidance I now need help rebuilding faith in.

It transpires this particular expression of frustration that spilled out of me frees up a lot of tension in me and others present. Experience of many years of these workshops has often shown me that total vulnerability and authenticity is healing, freeing and powerful. It's just not so fun when you are the one expressing it. However, a feeling of safety with Don and the group afforded me the opportunity and I feel less burdened in the wake of it.

A couple of men come to tell me over the next few days that they once were my son, so disillusioned with life that they made attempts to end their existence, but each were unsuccessful in their attempts and had learned much about themselves and changed things since the experience. One of these men, a young New Yorker of Iranian lineage called Nezam, and I form a strong bond over the weeks as he and I share the story from each side of the coin. It takes him a while to explain what intercepted and interrupted him at the last moment. Sensitive to the fact that I as a mother am struggling to come to terms with all of the feelings and fallout that my son's act unleashed, he takes his time to express the truth of what saved him.

'It was my mom,' he explains, searching for words that might not harm me. 'I couldn't imagine what it might do to her. She and I have a really good relationship,' he continues. 'I knew she would be devastated so I pulled back at the last second where choice remained possible.' His sensitivity in relating this to me is palpable as tears choke his words. Nezam relates how this personal hell brought him to greater self-awareness, and he found yoga, meditation and transforming cellular memory among other healing modalities that empowered him to change his life and helped him take charge of the anxiety and thoughts of worthlessness that plagued him.

Some days later, beads of perspiration multiply as I labour up the jungle path across the hill to a yoga class. I stumble upon a root and remind myself how the perilous terrain here causes me to stay completely in the moment. I am intercepted on the trail by Nezam, whom I have come to refer to as my Iranian prince, as he is making his way across to swim at the beach I live on. 'I am coming to find you, I thought you and I might go for a swim,' he says. In this instance, since I am already late for yoga, I decide to head back to the beach with him.

The rains had been heavy the evening before and the waves are stirred up. As I enter the water the current feels strong. He assures me when I get to the sandbank where he is, that it's very shallow, but the waves have other ideas. Before long I am out of my depth, there's no ground. The water crashes over me and swallowing, gulping, spluttering and flailing all over the place, there's a feeling of panic on me. 'Are you ok?' he yells over the din of waves crashing. 'No,' I splutter as I swallow yet more salty water. Nezam remains centred and calm and continually reassures me I am going to be OK. He makes a number of unsuccessful attempts to pull, push or guide me to safety. We are continually tossed and overcome with large crashing waves.

Meanwhile, a guy gestures frantically at the water's edge for us to swim to one side, away from the pull of the riptide. My futile attempts to swim exhaust me all the more. It comes to a point where I see my outstretched arm with Darragh's blue band reaching out. This is a rubber wristband with his name and musical notes on it, sported by all his friends. I grasp for my saviour's hand and then water takes me under again. There is a transparent watery blue-green wall in front of me and there is no sound. In that moment, I surrender. Here, time stops it seems, and an image of my childhood self fleets before me, followed by Ciara smiling at me as a toddler and then Darragh himself. I say to him in slow motion, 'It looks like it's my fate to join you son, from Thailand of all places.' Simultaneously, an abrupt question explodes in my head, 'What about your sister?' Again I see Ciara's face, this time as her nineteen-year-old self. In a split second, my Iranian prince grabs my arm and yanks me to the surface to air.

He has found his footing, he has ground beneath him and within seconds I too feel ground beneath my shaky feet. We stand clinging to each other as I wretch and cough water from my lungs. We make it to the shoreline and fall by the water's edge. My whole body goes numb followed by pins and needles, and all the while, I'm pushing water out of my lungs. The shoreline guy is over attending to us. I cannot speak as shock passes through my whole system. Slowly time regains perspective, breathing regulates and the enormity of the close call begins to take shape. I didn't lose consciousness or did I?

'Jeez, I thought there I was going to have to find your phone and call Derek and Ciara to tell them I lost you,' Nezam exclaims. 'That was one heck of a scary experience.'

Without warning or apology the most intense shame floods me. I ask my lifesaver not to look at me. 'What kind of stupid woman am I?' I blurt out. 'Creating a big drama like that, how weak am I?' My body is unable to hold me up as panic takes hold. I am so embarrassed. He presses me to tell him more of what I am feeling and he helps me get some perspective and make some sense of all that washes over me emotionally.

'Two people have drowned in this beach in similar circumstances over the past couple of years,' Nezam responds, 'so this is no mere drama queen having a moment. Why did you wait so long to alert me that you were in trouble? If I hadn't asked you would you have called for help?' He asks, 'Could this be indicative of a pattern in your life? Waiting until you are nearly drowning before you cry for help?' This gives me food for thought. Certainly, the title of 'helpless female' generates great shame in me.

After we regain our composure, we take a walk to the furthest point on the rocks and sit and observe the sea at its best. Wild and powerful as it crashes against the rocks spraying and foaming as the elements collide. He and I are quietly contemplating the scene before us, nature in its raw and wild passion. The intense almost catastrophic disaster making itself ever more present as we each recall another moment of wondering what the outcome might have been. After a time hunger kicks in, and we take ourselves ironically to the restaurant where I first landed, just weeks before, the place where I feared the decision to come here was a big mistake and here again I'm pondering the wisdom of the big adventure.

The four of us from the boat had remained in contact and often met for dinner in the first week or two of settling in. In fact, Charlotte and I spent time exploring the other side of the island together and had a few shopping trips to purchase sandals or sarongs of beautifully vibrant colours. Charlotte had only just recently moved on in the past few days as her boyfriend was joining her for the next leg of her travels on another island. Art had moved on too. He became a great jungle trekker, loving the challenge of the mountains and going it alone. He kept himself fit with his dance fests lasting hours at a time. Occasionally he and I would share a coconut and talk about our lives before this trip. He was a lawyer in Holland. I never would have guessed, as a suit would seem odd on his lean and well-developed muscular body. I never did get him those T-shirts, as he preferred to allow me to treat him to the occasional beer instead. He had grown up in Indonesia with parents who were very successful and busy and his earliest memories were of the help taking care of him. He shared with me how love and affection were not commonplace in his childhood. What incredibly interesting lives I am learning of in this place.

The last night the four of us spent together was quite magical and reminiscent of my teenage years. We had dinner sitting on the floor in our favourite restaurant, and later we joined a small group gathered on the beach. Daithí, living up to our nation's reputation, entertained the gathering with witty anecdotes and great stories. Songs and laughter permeated the stillness as we sat by a small fire under the moonlit sky. Some chose to swim in the dark waters, still warm even under the cover of night. I felt young and carefree in this experience, discovering a sense of lightness in me long forgotten.

After a coconut curry, Nezam and I make our way back to the beach. Upon our return, word has spread and we are surrounded by concerned and questioning friends. I want to be alone and escape the attention the episode of survival has generated. I wander along a quiet part of the beach alone and find myself not wanting to tell Ciara or Derek what happened. I have no desire to create fear or worry about my safety or well-being among those so far from me physically and so close emotionally.

Derek and I are struggling to feel any level of connection as Wi-Fi is unreliable here. Our intimate level of communicating is being greatly hampered and is usually our strong point. We have, in fact, pulled back our contact as our worlds are so remarkably different. As

I sit in contemplation under the stars, a soft warm breeze caressing my shoulders and back like a light shawl protecting me, it begins to dawn on me. I have to let go even of my relationship with Derek. He says he's happy without me as he is getting to be with himself and reconnect with a part of him that has been lost in relationships and parenting for twenty years. Whilst I understand the sentiment of what he is saying as I too am finding an inner me long since buried, I also know that I am attached to us being something. 'Is there anything of my old life I can keep?' I say out loud into the darkness. 'Who am I now – if not the mother at home with her teenagers; if not the tutor or social care worker; if not the healer and if not the lover or partner; then who?'

I realise that I have become too invested in the idea of us, the wonderful love story of best friends becoming life partners in the face of adversity and pain; the story where love wins the day. Unsure of what is winning this day, I retire to my cabin.

Chapter 19
Where to call home?

~

L ife breathes through my body on the daily crossing of the jungle path, over the hill, to meet my new friends, while I sit in my hammock watching the boats or when I attend a yoga class. However, in the build-up to departing exotic-island living, my focus is on home.

What will that feel like? How will it be to hug and hold my loved ones? My relationship is now in doubt as the physical distance has continued impacting significantly on us. Our conversations are often strained and feel disconnected. It feels like a lot is at stake and all of it uncertain.

I am watching a group of young party revellers and remembering the freedom of youth, wanting and wishing for Darragh to have travelled and experienced some of life as these young people are doing. I leave them to their young carefree existence and hedonism and wander along a short, beautiful but empty beach. Thinking of him with yearning in my heart and simultaneously feeling appreciation for the experience and vista, I feel a tingling along my hand like the brushing of a gentle breeze. I know it is him walking alongside me from his new place. It has that sparkly quality that comes when he is near, and it feels exquisite and beautiful and oh, so painful too, as his physical absence becomes ever more real. I walk in slow steady steps, feeling this mix of intense emotions, and stop where the beach ends. I face the water, illuminated in sparkling lines by the moon, to tell him how I miss his physicality.

A rustle behind me brings my awareness back and out of the shrubbery walks a friend from home, Eoin, who is here with his girlfriend, Cathy, both of whom I know. Eoin is another great support to me here, and me to him, as we settle in to a completely transformed way of living. He embraces me warmly as if he knows exactly what is required in the moment; no words are necessary as on some level he knows what is going on. A beautiful moment sent to me by Darragh from beyond the divide.

The departure date comes up fast and the last days are spent in great appreciation of the place and people that have crossed my path. Sitting on a wooden platform under the stars, guitar music and song wafting over me, the last evening couldn't be better. A collection of amazing people and I are swapping life philosophies, shared moments and contact details.

A small posse waves me off from the shoreline the following morning. My lifesaver, Nezam, presents me with an amulet pouch, hand-made by him, containing a beach stone. This touches me somewhere deep inside. reminding me of the unexplainable deep connection that we share. He and I and the very tall Liverpudlian, Stefano, formed an eclectic trio as we wandered from beach to beach, eating in one of the four or five choices of restaurants; each of us sharing, in a deep and meaningful way, our life experiences. Stefano, with his strong accent particular to that part of England, had a favourite pastime of asking for five random words which he then turned into a poem which was relevant to you and characteristically accurate. The level of creativity in his mind is a joy and is fascinating to get an insight into. He sees the world in moving, colourful images and shares his visions. He and Nezam are bosom buddies, often laughing so hysterically that people ask me what drugs they are taking. 'Life,' I would regularly reply to incredulous faces. Surely no one can be that happy. Lost soulmates who have found each other, was my explanation for their inextricable close bond.

Stefano presents me with a card and a fish-shaped stone. Tears spring as I read his wonderful words thanking me for our weeks of learning together. Love fills me for these people who have touched my heart and soul, for this place and for the rich, albeit not always pleasant, experiences. Ungracefully as ever, I clamber on board the ferry away from the most incredible surreal experience, home to another surreal reality. It turns out this was the perfect place to find some healing.

The trip home is smooth enough, and I enjoy the adventure of the travel as long as my mind is not wandering home before me, asking unanswerable questions. Will home feel like home after six weeks away? Will my love life be reignited? How has Ciara really fared out? Slight rumblings of panic are forming at the edges of my mind about life as I left it. It has been all grand and adventurous for me cavorting halfway around the world, but now this is a reality check. My re-emergence into what was familiar is feeling ambiguous to say the least. I comfort myself with the feeling that I have retrieved a part of myself long since lost. This part of me will surely help with the re-entry.

A missed last connecting flight means Ciara cannot make the airport, so my beloved Derek is the only one waiting. When we see each other it is as if he is the only person in the arrivals hall. My whole being is happy to see him and we embrace in a long, heart-connected, love-filled hold. My body and soul breathes a sigh of relief as I know in this moment we are OK, we are good. 'I love you,' he whispers into my hair and I know it is true. That strange magic reignites. We are transported into a bubble of love. All around us, sounds begin to melt and fade. Laughter, voices, the sound of wheels grating on the floor as trolleys and wheelie bags pass us by, seem to intermingle with the general din, yet disappear into the distance. He shines in the coffee queue as I sit and wait at a white tabletop, shiny from the damp cloth that has just wiped it clean. It is as if his inner light is switched on to me and mine to him, a feeling reminiscent of the kiss that wasn't a kiss moment from those years ago in the park. Whatever else follows there is an internal sigh of relief flooding me.

Derek drives me to meet Ciara, and I natter incessantly, realising I haven't been in a car for six weeks. When we reach our street, home seems so far away, not in the physical sense, but when I come through the door it feels like I am detached from the place. It's a house and the fresh paint from the house revamp does enhance the experience, but the space has no feeling of life or homeliness.

It's so good to reconnect with Ciara. Again the embrace tells a lot and I realise she really has been OK in my absence. She confesses that she spends little or no time in the house and finds our little town difficult to be in – too many anchors, too many memories. I know this for myself. I go to buy petrol and the kind shop assistant asks from her heart, 'How are getting on? I think of you often.' We both fill with tears as I reply. And so re-emergence feels conflicting despite such happiness to reconnect with all those I missed and missed me. Derek and I spend the first weekend by the sea just north of Dublin in Carlingford Lough, where his friend has offered us a house. This affords us space and time and brings so much reconnection between us and consolidates the feeling at the airport. It's as if not only our love and life connection from the past few years is consolidated but a deeper, older, other-worldly, past-life feeling is strong and evidenced both in our physical intimacy and in the emotional resonance we naturally occupy. A touch electrifies, a smile nudges the heart into repair and love and laughter fill the two days.

The journey back home this time after that lovely distraction for those couple of days to what was a once happy house is tough. No one is waiting; no fanfare or welcome committee. Feelings of fear and reticence fill me. Most of me wants to run back to Thailand or back by the sea in Carlingford to that lovely bubble of love where in a moment Darragh's absence is not the main feature. Anywhere but where I am heading. Back to reality; that is what looms. This turning of the key in the door feels so raw, so lonely. The celebrity attention of being away and back is gone. Who knew I would enjoy such attention? Now it's just me, the empty space and uncertainty.

Special leave is still activated, as it is still term time. Now the honeymoon of my return fades as life resumes as normal and I am left to face the fact that there is no income. The travel fund is almost gone, no entitlement exists while on leave and the situation looks bleak. Enlisting the help of Louise, the artist in our family, a flyer is designed and printed at her expense. I begin to advertise and try to build my one-on-one clients. This is a slow process and despite my best attempts to manage, my dwindling fund is gone. I get a call to do some work with a young woman whom I barely know, a friend of Louise. She is in a city hospital with an unclear diagnosis. Early, on my journey to work with her, my car begins to splutter and behave strangely. Before I know it I find myself stopped in the lashing rain at the side of the road, with no spark in the engine at all. Attempts to call Kevin, my daughter's mechanic boyfriend, come to nothing. In fact no one is available, and for a time I sit there with rivulets of rain on the windscreen matching the tears on my face. Here I sit, broken on so many levels, and the future feels foreboding.

This is a material world and everyone I know has already contributed so much time and resources to me it is embarrassing to think about. After years of independence, albeit close to the wind trying to support two children with occasional support from my loving family and a particular friend who always contributed to Christmas, here I find myself on the side of the road, with no means to live on and with a vehicle that could bring me to a client, now clapped out. How can life be so cruel? I am a good person. I value my friends and family. I work hard. What has happened to my life?

The devastation I feel is totally disproportionate to a broken-down car. I sit in it until a passer-by stops and knocks on the window, bringing me back to the moment. He tries to jump-start the engine but is unsuccessful and leaves me waiting a while longer for Derek to come and tow me home.

A few days later, Kevin has fixed the car up for free. The alternator was the problem. Alternating from life in Thailand to life in Ireland, is that what it reflects? Things are looking no brighter though, and I try to hatch a plan to generate some income. I know my days living in our home are numbered. The banks need payments, my arrangement with them has timed out so as the house is in negative equity renting makes the most sense. I begin to try and get my mind into this idea. Discussion with Ciara is paramount. I suggest she and Kevin move in and rent a room to another young couple. However, she is very clear; she cannot even consider living there anymore. I feel trepidation about the house not being available to us, to her in particular. It's one thing to choose not to sleep in the house where you lived with your family after a tragedy, but quite another not to be able to stop in and make tea, sit in his room, be in your own room or call in to see your mother in the space you call home.

All of this weighs heavily on me as I try in the meantime to drum up a source of income. Within a short space of time, the trip away feels like a distant dream and home feels like an anchor caught on a rock. Little by little, I start clearing out stuff that's no longer of use. It amazes me how much the three of us have accumulated. It also does not escape me that I am moving easy stuff, superfluous to daily life. Nothing from his room yet! Nothing that holds a memory or triggers a remembering of any kind!

The days pass and the money issue grows; one cannot leave the house without some. I muster up the courage to ask a friend for a loan with a repayment plan based on the rental income having a very modest profit. She gracefully declines and I find myself so discouraged. I feel like a liability. Yes, I can do lunch if you pay. Days later she does offer me a car that her infirm aunt cannot drive anymore so it won't be used again. I can sell or drive it. Based on my recent car experience I agonise over the choice. It is a few years older than mine but with fewer miles on the clock. The decision to sell comes and I borrow from my partner on the strength of it selling, which takes a frustratingly long time. Nonetheless, I am extremely grateful for the gift, as at least I have breathing space now, financially.

Eventually I do get to the woman in hospital and we have a beautiful session. Her body is so weak from surgery and drugs, and her daily struggle with pain puts my woes into perspective. I get to feel a really lovely connection with her and in that first session I know I cannot charge her as her finances mirror mine somewhat. Between her sister and Louise they offer to cover costs for more sessions to follow. Both this woman and I are blessed with gems as sisters. The diagnosis, when it does come, is terminal, and she lives but a few months more. Once again I feel the paradox of pain and love. My time with her is precious and valued by me and herself and her loved ones, and it seems part of my role becomes to help ease her into the next world.

She moves home from the hospital with a team of medical support and a rota of helpers and minders consisting of family and friends. Some make nutritious smoothies for her to drink, others prop her up so that she can enjoy the view of her beautiful roses waving in the wind outside her cottage window. During my visits she often lets go and surrenders into a deep relaxation. On one such occasion she seems to come back briefly and whispers to me, 'I see you with a pen! Are you writing?' To my astounded, 'Yes,' she replies, 'It is important, keep going,' and then she drifts off again. On some visits she talks about her fear of dying, the injustice of having so much left to do with her life, her recent engagement proposal from her partner now unlikely to be realised. 'I can talk to you about all this stuff,' she says, 'because you won't stress and fret about it. I don't want to worry my family and friends.'

I am blessed to feel her spirit as it prepares to leave and it is the most exquisite, rich, beautiful experience. I am sitting in a meditation healing circle with a small group and I am brought to see her long flowing hair, long since disappeared after chemotherapy, in a field of the most beautifully coloured flowers. She is so vibrant and alive and smiling with her whole being. I am blown away by this image and find myself overwhelmed with such joy and love for all in the group. It's hard to contain or put words on. Nuggets of wisdom flow as if through me for each of the group and I pass them on as best I can. I bask in this glow for the rest of that evening. She leaves her physical body a few hours later with her nearest and dearest beside her bed and her close friends sitting together in her artist's studio at the back of her house, holding each other in loving support as they listen to songs and share stories of her.

Her funeral, like Darragh's, is reflective of her unique personality and wonderful artistic talents, and it is so heartbreaking as those who love her say goodbye. The recounting of her friends' escapades to obtain marigolds, her favourite flowers, for her coffin provides a welcome tension relief. They managed to get a bathtub full and her coffin was overflowing with crimson, orange and yellow leaves cascading over the sides. Louise's friend has now also departed before her time it would seem. 'I have so much grief stored up inside me,' Louise says, in the days following, 'I am not sure how to access or express it. How can life bring so many cruel twists of fate?'

Chapter 20
Time to move on

The experience of being with someone in their last days and at their most vulnerable stays with me for a time after she has moved on. I feel privileged to be trusted at such a deep level and simultaneously upset at the injustice of a woman in her prime having to leave the world as her body gives up at thirty-six years of age. I do some work with a couple of her friends, Louise included, as they try to make sense of it all. This involves sitting in a safe space with each person individually and tuning in to their energy field, either by putting my hands on their energy centres or just listening to the energy under the words and feelings they express. I can help them express and clear the emotions they have in relation to their friend's death. Guilt, frustration and helplessness seem to be predominant feelings. Fear for their own mortality, the question of life and the meaning we give it are thrown into the neutral zone as a way of releasing.

Whilst I know there is more than just this world, as Louise's friend and Darragh have shown me, it remains challenging when a life seems unfinished. Of course we are measuring with our societal conditioned belief systems which tell us that this is an unfinished life, when in terms of spirit, this is completion at this level, or so I have come to believe. Otherwise the spirit would remain. How can it be that some are here and lying in hospital beds without the ability to communicate or fend for themselves at all, dependent on medical staff and interventions, old and infirm. Are they doing soul work still? Can we judge anyone's quality of life using our own filter and conditioned beliefs that say, in order to be fulfilled you must adhere to certain criteria? Some with such seemingly difficult paths inspire and teach so many. However, some days it is hard to see how any of these early departures from life can be positive, especially when viewed from this one-dimensional human level, which seems to be the way of it for me, especially since my return from Thailand.

Day-to-day life has an underlying feeling of loneliness. People come in and out of my daily experience as before, but I find it hard to connect. I am burdened by my own world of heavy responsibility. How can they know what this feels like? My focus is on finding a way to let go of all that has been my connection to life as a mother in that day-to-day requirement that existed within these four walls. I am packing to go somewhere. I don't know where, as still I live without means. I try not to discuss or focus on the lack as it feels like a challenge too great to overcome. My very helpful friends are all consumed with their own responsibilities, and so I feel like I am dragging a ship around after me and my mind cannot understand why in the face of all that is before me, this extra pressure financially has to be.

I tell myself how lucky I am that I got to spend time away as I did. So many live this tragedy with no escape, without friends who rally around to support, like mine do. But the feeling is very strong that I have cashed in my support chips. How can living be so expensive? Everything is at a cost. The contrast is exacerbated by the really cheap cost of living in the East that I so recently experienced. I try to manage the loan from my partner as best I can and continue to pack. Louise has offered me a room with her an hour or so away from where I live and an extra hour from Derek's. I know my relationship with both her and Lisa is really good and it is a real possibility. Derek and I discuss me moving in with him but we both know it doesn't feel like that's right for us yet.

However, my mood is low and it is taking more of my strength and so much of my resources, built up over many years, to get through another day and to fill another box. This decision about where to go can wait. Eventually I take the bull by the horns, and with Ciara's support, we declare the house for rent. Interestingly, within a week, a dad of one of his crew calls me with a tenant he can vouch for and give a reference to, as he is his employer. This is such great news. This is a family with young twin girls, and I know immediately the house needs that life and noise back into its space. The rent will cover the house payments without much change but at least the banks will be off my back. Now the time frame has been set, I have six weeks to get moved. Suddenly the pressure is on. No more melancholic long days of feeling sorry for myself, not that they don't happen, but I now have motivation to get things done. I am offered a storage space in a friend's shed for some stuff that she is happy to keep for as long as I need.

Ciara and I nominate a time to do his room. We are both dreading the task. It is decidedly difficult to put words on such a job, but we hold ourselves well in it. Memories flooding us as we unpack shelves, drawers, wardrobes, discerning the 'must haves', we each make a pile. Tears flow and laughter erupts as we uncover over days so many good times and memories of him. 'Do you remember the day when we went … and he …' is the most frequently used sentence. From his favourite bedtime storybooks to his first painting at school, his school reports, drumsticks, football socks, his hair gel still standing on his chest of drawers – what to do with each and every object is discussed, evaluated and placed in a corresponding pile. In this room, the keepsake piles are greater. Seemingly insignificant things now hold paramount value.

With so many trips to the charity shops and the landfill, it beggars belief how much stuff gets accrued over years. A deep sigh of relief is my overriding feeling when his room finally gets done. His life is now contained in a number of precious boxes as is his sister's and mine. What to keep with me in my new, likely to be, Louise and Lisa's spare room? How much do I need? Ornaments, photos, books, music, CDs, videos, DVDs, pictures, candles and so much memorabilia from our lives as a family. Overwhelming stuff everywhere!

His bedroom furniture carries his memory. I can't leave it behind, even though it will end up in a shed indefinitely, so it gets a storage sticker for now. All shelves, cupboards, drawers and spaces have to be cleared out. I work steadily most days alone, with Ciara in and out doing her part with her things, but no one can decide for me what carries sentiment or not. I have been consistently progressing in my ability to get on with the task in hand and not get too caught in the why, the where to next, the injustice, the upset and the fear.

Some days bring more frustrated crying than others. The worst avalanche occurs when I am amidst the clearing of the bed linen from the hot press. Reaching up above my head, I pull a cascade of pillowcases down on top of myself. One from Darragh's bed is the last one to land and it is like the last straw. All my brave resolve, all my stoicism crumbles, and I hear myself disintegrating as sound escapes from deep within me. The reel of film begins in my head, not for the first time, as scenes from our lives fill my mind without apology or pause. Time ceases to exist as I am overcome with deep feelings that barely allow for breath to flow. All consuming, the enormity of his act and the subsequent consequences invade every cell. We are packing up that whole chapter of our lives. All of me knows that this has to be the next step but I'm struggling to exist in the midst of the confusion and despair. All of my being wants life back the way it was. The impossible wish of a grieving mother!

My way back from this precipice of devastation comes in a most insane way. Derek puts on a swimming cap that tumbles in the pile and finds me a matching one. He plonks it on my head. Suddenly the ridiculousness of us sitting on the floor in that strangely named part of the house, 'the landing,' between bedrooms, amidst a pile of bed linen and a random collection of beach wear, the total senselessness takes precedence and laughter ensues. That thin line between despair and insanity ever thinner and laughter acting as a catalyst in this instance as it has many times before, breaking the process of grief and interrupting the pattern to allow another feeling to emerge.

As the departure date draws closer, the support group of helpers grows until eventually the day comes and the van arrives. Derek drives me and my valuables to various places of storage. The last night in the house feels strange, as many items of furniture remain, but it is as if the personality of the space has been stripped bare. Ciara comes to say her goodbye to each room and cannot be persuaded to stay. I find myself after she leaves walking around thanking the rooms and the space for the family life and memories we have had there. I acknowledge the freshness of a new family coming to occupy the place and make their stamp on the décor and create their feeling in the place. The doorbell rings. Darragh's crew file in. They know we are moving, each one in their own version of feeling as this is the last time for them to be in this space.

They comment on how it looks so similar, but feels so different. A lot of the furniture remains but the space is so devoid of sentimental items that it bears little resemblance to what they knew. Darragh's large-framed photo, now standing by the couch ready to come with me, is moved to various seats as we playfully ask him who he wants to sit beside, and generally, this creates plenty of amusement. A need to visit his room seems to be evident as one asks, 'Can we go to his room for one more visit?' They bound up the stairs to gather in the now empty space. Again they seem so large in the small space, and we stand around the walls and try to take in and integrate the change. The common theme seems to be that this just isn't right, space being empty and his stuff packed up. 'This is just wrong,' one of them says, summing up the vibe. 'This house is supposed to stay the same for us to come in and remember.'

It is duly noted that the stars or spit wads have disappeared from the ceiling, and they enjoy discussing pens firing wads of paper in school and how Darragh always got caught. No matter who else was involved, he took the rap. Most all of them now have an item or two of his in their possession that they have a particular memory or association of him attributed to. Although they are moving on, this house brings all of them back to another time, only a year and a half ago, when they were regulars calling most days in short bursts of activity and on again. It's a double-edged sword, pain and pleasure in one moment.

The evening unfolds in the more usual kind of interaction; tea-making, jokes and storytelling, music, dancing, singing, the door open and shutting as smokes are had outside in the garden or calls are made. So much makes me laugh out loud – the country song mimed by one with a hat of mine as a prop; the throwing of the hula hoop to see whose head can catch it; the recounting of the time Darragh jumped the wall only to break his collarbone and how the crew knew he was in trouble by the strange sound that escaped his lips; the Ed Sheeran song performed as many times before by three of them, not a word missed now as they have practised often.

Eventually after a long photo shoot and lots of tea, it's time for us all to part company – me, their friends' mam and they, the maturing lads and young women, joined together by the adversity of such loss that it cannot be easily expressed in words. Again music and song provides us with a common ground where we can meet. Their noisy departure and promises of visits to my sister's side of the country leaves me shell-shocked and so, so lonely. Standing in the kitchen again, the sink overflowing with mugs and cups, the loud silence makes itself known to me. I'm so unsure what to do with myself. It seems too late to ring Derek. Minutes later, without warning, the front door bursts open and the crew rush in and surround me in a mass group hug. 'Group hug, group hug,' they chant, as they swamp me, all of them so much taller than I. 'We thought you might be feeling sad,' they declare. How wonderful are these young people.

Once again they completely astound me with their sensitivity. It feels encouraging to me, for the future of our race, that these young people can be so understanding and sensitive in the face of their own experience, grappling with the aftermath of their friend's atomic bomb of an act. Although the tears cannot be avoided and the silence is ever louder again when they leave, sleep comes surprisingly easily that last night in that little house in the cul-de-sac, where little ones continue to have tea parties on the grass and lads kick ball and wrestle, and life goes on for the rest of the world of family. One of the crew changes their Facebook profile the next morning to his picture with me; a bemused Ciara rings to inform me.

Chapter 21
Into the unknown

The first weeks in Louise's feel good. It's the height of summer and their home is situated on a tourist trail that is steeped in history. Thanks to the medieval castle, beautiful grounds, walks, rivers, trinket shops to browse in, an endless array of good cafés to frequent and their dog needing walks, my days seem to be filled.

Writing has become a focus and provides a sense of purpose for me. An underlying feeling of relief is emerging as the big job of getting out of the house is done. The wonderful new tenants love the place and despite my only having little money and a room in another's living space that bulges with all my precious necessities, I can be in the busy streets and observe the world or retreat to the nature spots or that room that feels like my cave.

Louise and Lisa are often away from home and are sensitive and caring when they return. We manage easily to share the living space. Time is interspersed with visits to Derek's and friends or them to me. However, it is not long before another feeling starts to become loud in its presence. The novelty factor wears thin and I begin to question my purpose and existence. Almost half a century old, my life has been reduced to living in my sister's spare room. The lack of finances weighs on me. Efforts to establish myself as a therapist in the area have brought me to meet a lovely bunch of people who swop treatments with me, but few paying clients emerge.

Trips to Derek's are almost impossible to fuel. My hair needs a cut so badly I'm embarrassed to ask for any more loans. I try my luck at social welfare again. Until my leave is over or I return to work part-time, there's nothing for me. I ask at the local café where there is a 'Help Wanted' sign displayed, and I'm unceremoniously told I'm too old. 'I need someone fast on the floor and with barista experience,' she says, eyeing me in a non-complimentary way, before adding, 'Of course, you are welcome to leave a CV.' I'm almost indignant at the rebuke. Am I now that aged that the young supervisor thinks I wouldn't make the grade? Indignation fades to deflation in a matter of moments.

And so my street walking becomes a job search and tourists seem to have it all worked out. Armed with umbrellas for the short bursts of showers, they are out and about under the cloudy sky with layers of thin clothing for protection against the chill that comes as soon as a cloud covers the sun. Ice creams, cameras and maps in hand, these families remind me of days gone by. 'Treasure these moments,' I say to them but only in my mind. I do wish that they can enjoy and feel happiness in every moment they share.

The thing that makes most sense to me currently is writing. Here time disappears as my story flows out, bringing me to tears in many instances as I replay the last year and a half over and over. So I continue to write. Ruth, a friend from work whose unwavering support got me through many tough days in that environment and whose shed holds my worldly possessions, is visiting me in my new home and asks can I send her my words. Nervously I concede. The feedback is so positive, practical and helpful. She asks how I have survived thus far. What is in my emergency toolkit that gets me through even the most awful moments?

And so I reflect on what is getting me through the mire. What is it that I am doing? Humour ironically plays a major role. Who could imagine laughter in the face of such trauma? Yet, in my family, with friends and with Derek, it supports me so often in the midst of emotion. Darragh, the ultimate joker, loved entertaining his sister, me, his friends and anyone who may have paused long enough to get to know him. His regular bum-shake dance to our phone ringtone was impossible not to laugh at. His interpretation of an accent, thrown into regular daily activities, always brought light into the house.

On one occasion, Louise and I, on her insistence, buy swimming goggles for 'the crying' and wrap them up as gifts for each member of the family, including grandparents. We pass them around and laughter erupts as everyone unwraps the spontaneous gift and models them. Here we are a family plunged into despair, sitting around the dinner table looking insanely ridiculous, laughing and crying as we look around at the distortion in each face as the goggles pull the skin tight around our eyes. It feels bizarre and sounds almost not becoming of a family in grief, yet the laughter and tears balancing so precariously on a very thin line does bring a moment's reprieve even in the early days.

Many of my inner circle continue to treat me as before, calling for advice on parenting or other issues. 'I need your advice about setting a boundary for my teenager who is driving me up the wall,' the exasperated voice of Helen comes down the phone and I am so relieved; relieved she is carrying on our friendship as before as we share parenting tips, relieved she obviously still values my opinion in this arena, relieved she doesn't see me as a failure as a parent and relieved that I am not treated like porcelain.

For some, porcelain is the only way they can see me, as I wrestle with most parents' worst nightmare. I feel the angst in their uncertainty in how to be around me. Many are afraid to discuss their own issues as they feel them minimised in the face of my burden. I can be a liability to be around. I could be overcome with a flood of grief, and while I can support myself in this for the most part, for some it's just a challenge to be in my company. The feeling of helplessness permeates amongst those who would love to help.

And so many incredible and wonderful things do come my way. A fellow therapist Su, training in a new modality, offers me an unending run of treatments and, suffering with a frozen shoulder, this is a fantastic support to my physical healing. When some of my inner circle realise I am short the cash for a haircut, an appointment is booked and paid for.

Another real unexpected support has come from experiencing

what I believe to be evidence of another plane of existence. Many examples come through different people and channels and these bring me much curiosity and some reprieve of pain. I feel like it's him trying to get through to me any way he can.

One Monday morning, not long after my return to work, I have a meeting with a student, a man in his fifties who is upskilling, after years of ill health and nursing his incapacitated mother had kept him out of the workforce. It is a routine check about an assignment, to see how it is progressing for him. He is obvious in his discomfort as we are coming to the end of our conversation and he shuffles on his seat. It's a hard-backed, plastic chair, particularly uncomfortable for this large-framed man. He asks if it's appropriate to share an experience he had after the funeral. He recounts that upon retiring to bed that evening he saw his bedroom fill up with light and he felt himself to be so incredibly happy and loved. He says that although he didn't know Darragh nor had the opportunity of meeting him, he was very clear in the moment that it was him. 'I will never forget the experience,' he says, 'it was so incredible and beautiful.'

His eyes and mine fill with tears as he tells me this extraordinary story, and again I am both moved and grateful for the courage it evidently took for this man to share with me. He had feared it might have posed too much of an emotional push on me in the workspace. 'Thank you,' I say, 'for giving me a gift in sharing your story, reminding me that he is not gone, just transformed.' I smile tearfully and leave the classroom enthralled by the magic of that encounter.

Creaking floors in my home were a repeated nuisance. One particularly noisy night, I sat up and wondered if it was next door or my imagination playing tricks? Was it a throwback of wishful thinking, as when we lived as a family, often a late-night wander for a drink or toilet visit would cause such noise? The answer comes the following day. Another student comes to me after class and tells me she has had a visit from my son. This young vibrant woman has an intensely busy home life with a young family and a sibling with special needs whom she helps to take care of. She clutches a handwritten note. 'Some messages that he wants you to know. I used to see spirits all the time,' she says, 'but I had to stop them coming to me as it was too much. Everybody wanted me to tell them things, get messages from their loved ones.' She speaks as if she is talking about a retail shop she used to buy clothes in and since stopped, as if seeing spirits all the time is the most natural thing in the world. For some, I guess that is true. I am reminded of the fortune teller woman I picked up that Saturday, not long after he died.

'I had to make an exception for you,' she continues, 'after all you are my favourite tutor and he was very persistent. Was he like that in real life?' she inquires. I nod quite vigorously, remembering how he could be like a dog with a bone if he wanted something, asking over and over again as to the why of things if the answer was not to his liking. I'm pretty spellbound already by what I am hearing.

She begins to read her notes. She tells me that they were written as an agreement to get him to leave her bedroom at 3 a.m. I nearly want to pinch myself to see if I am really awake and sitting in the common room at work. 'The creaking floors last night were him,' she reveals. I am blown away! I consider myself very open to the possibility of communication with the other realm, having experienced moments of feeling other-worldly presences come often in a session with someone, but this level of clear communication he is having with such an eclectic mix of people is unprecedented. This student is talking of really personal details of my life not possible for her to know. She says he understands now the importance of the ring I always wear and supports that sentiment in me. I'm reeling now trying to make sense of the information. My ring, the ring I bought for myself when my marriage was well and truly over, was to reclaim 'me' again after nearly twenty years in a relationship.

She says he loves the funeral we created, a recurring comment from him; he loves the personal touch and especially the musical presence of his crew. He says he is watching out for all of his close mates and crew. She says he is so free now and loves us all. Needless to say, in that exchange, my mind is reeling and somewhat bewildered by this accurate spontaneous reading.

His childhood friend is visiting us with his parents and tells me that a few days prior to their visit, he felt himself being shoved in the shoulder. He turned around to rebuke the perpetrator only to find there was no one behind him. He also speaks of waking in the night and feeling a presence, Darragh's presence, in the room. Freaked out, he called to his brother next door who was having the same experience. The crew speak of lights in their homes behaving strangely; 'flicking on and off for no good reason,' the car driver of the group said.

One of Darragh's football coaches recounts to me in tears, 'That fella is still a messer. My computer has got a mind of its own these days,' he says, 'switching itself on and off with no one near it.' He is convinced that Darragh is fiddling with their electrics and computer. This man has a big, open wound in his heart, and was one of the first on the scene that fateful day. I will never forget the look on his face as he tried to shield me from the scene behind him. This man, who had walked by that exact tree the night before with his dog and a torch, was now unable to comprehend what the next morning's search brought to light. He was a strong support to my son, noticing his best qualities, reminding him he was a good enough player on the pitch, something Darragh was not always so sure of. This man and his wife continue to be a major support for many of the young people in the community. He, having lived with his own brother's suicide, knows only too well the pain it causes.

In the early days, the list was continually expanding as people recounted their own experiences of what they perceived to be his influence. One evening as I sit in a group for meditation and healing, I feel a big expanse of light envelope me as if uplifting me with it. I know it's him from some other part of me that has now been switched on. Suddenly we are at his school and I see the vast fog of light burst through the building, exploding out the windows and then swooping out over the town across the canal and river and back to me there in the group. I felt as if the whole town received a message, a healing from him, that I felt privileged to be part of. Dreaming, imagining, experiencing? Whatever it is, it feels wonderful and a total contrast to the loss and desolation.

Ciara, the night before an exam, was anxious and unable to settle her mind. She was lying in bed and described feeling a trickle on her back followed by a warm feeling all over and a sense of being tucked in. She recalls feeling so protected and loved. 'I knew it was going to be OK, Mam,' she says. 'It was like he was telling me not to worry and get some sleep.' Considering that exam was only three weeks after he left us, it is a miracle she sat it at all never mind passed it, but she did.

Derek awakens one morning at 5 a.m. beside me. I'm lying there already awake and he is overcome with a joyous expression of love and compassion that he can barely contain. Through his tears and upset, I see and feel a love that bears a quality not of this world, and he tells me that where Darragh is, is amazing and magical and beyond our wildest dreams. 'How can I tell you what this feels like? It's beyond words and so beautiful,' he splutters almost incoherently as emotion floods him. I don't need words. It's infectious and I feel it so strongly. We sit up in bed in the darkened room and bask in this glow of incandescent light, and I know in my heart it's him, Darragh, trying once again to give me a glimpse of what it feels like from beyond the divide. Me, living on the edge of despair, gleaning a moment of reprieve through this beautiful, poignant moment shared with my partner.

I'm sitting in the cinema with an empty seat beside me. I love to have an empty seat nearby where I can imagine Darragh, sitting there with me. Watching *The Hobbit*, enthralled and captivated by the wondrous scenes that fill the screen of distant magical lands almost floating in the sky. Ethereal, the special effects are captivating and fuel my imagination. This is underscored by the magical music that creates opportunity for my soul to open and be touched. Here, he and I can meet in the midst of a packed cinema. Maybe just maybe the world he experiences now resembles the wondrous scenes that fill the screen. I feel joyful. As the film ends, I remain slightly detached from the world. It's as if I observe it from a far off distant place, filled with a love for all that is before me, irrespective of their activities. Is this love coming from me or from him through me or just some moment of delusion? I carry it with me out to the night sky of the carpark and way on into the rest of that evening.

'If only we could all live from this place,' I say to a smiling Derek.

But this is not an exceptional, once-off incident. I know when this happens to me or through Derek it's an insight into another way of being. In that place, for those moments, I judge no one and feel only love and the space to allow everyone and everything to be exactly as they are in that moment.

Extraordinary as those incidences sound, they really help get me through another moment of another day. These precious moments in time are what help in the face of the awfulness that an act like his brings about. They show up any time, any place, anywhere. My struggle to come to terms with, make sense of, try and get some clarity on, is an ongoing, daily requirement with some days taking an easier route than others. The uncensored questioning of myself and the 'What if's?' are an unsatisfying torment resulting in me falling down the emotional scale to despair and disillusionment. In another moment I can reframe these questions and ask what can I do in the face of this? How can I help myself or someone else? What, in this moment, could I do to make this feel easier? Then the challenge is to go with whatever comes in the moment. Hence, the breakfast in the local café that gave me a connection with the medium needing a lift.

Showing up to salsa dance class is sometimes a blessing, in that the music, the anonymity, the need to focus on the new step and follow the lead of the male is such a mind distraction. I can almost forget my predicament for a moment or ten minutes or on occasion for a whole class. Naturally in some instances this would all be too much and a hasty exit is the only escape. A need to walk in the park, sit on a bench and let the waves of feelings wash over me, or walk along the seafront is all that is possible as the flow of emotion is too great to sidestep or distract from.

The challenge then is to get back to class the following week, my mind suggesting that it's all a waste of time as nothing will ever be of value to me again. 'Why bother with this nonsense?' I hear in my head. Luckily Derek is also at the class which is an incentive in itself, but nonetheless everything that was normal or fun is now etched with a new unstable foundation. My feet are in quicksand and the frivolity of dance class is sometimes more than I can bear. Some moments I wish the only thing that posed a worry is whether the step is executed correctly or not. In other moments I want to scream, 'Who cares? It's not so important.'

Another one of the most healing things for me to move out of pain and also come into my body is making love. Connecting intimately is a joy, to feel love and passion even in the midst of pain, loss and despair. How can I feel and express and enjoy love in the midst of such pain? How can it be that I could allow love blossom to the extent that it has unfolded? We, a couple in the midst of exploring the possibility of really changing our friendship, and taking our time to do so, now have become an incredible love story. That inexplicable paradox that exists in life, where pain and pleasure coexist in a moment separated only by a hair's breadth, a thought, a decision often made in the unconscious.

From the outset of this experience, somewhere in me a decision was made to live in the face of his death – to live after him, not to wither and die after him. I decide every day in every moment to heal the gaping wound that is my heart; broken open, torn inextricably apart in a way one cannot even imagine. I live now in a way that takes up the goalposts as I move and tries replacing and resetting new ones as I go. It's disconcerting, it's ever-changing, it's insecure and unpredictable and I am learning to move with it.

My conditioned beliefs and supports, the learning I was born into and raised through doesn't really serve me. I had already been questing to find answers. I set upon this voyage of discovery long before his act and yet his act has catapulted me ever more into questioning, unravelling and rebuilding. With my belief systems stripped bare, back to the foundations, I begin again weeding out the beliefs, traditions and societal points of reference that don't serve my healing. Instead, I lean in the direction of love and support that feels right, where my heightened instincts lead me.

I know I have to feel all of it. Synchronicity often brings me to a healing session or workshop that will help. Already open and working in balancing energy has given me tremendous relief and support. Numbing with drink or drugs is not a choice I can make. I've spent too long cultivating a way of opening up to feelings. Some days, nature in all of its raw beauty and capacity to be of itself, following some intrinsic unfolding of its intended purpose, is the only reprieve I can find.

A sustained noticing of the blessing of love that I experience so much around me is like a blanket of support woven for me by my friends and family, members of my community and his crew, just by their very being in their true teenage selves. Human thoughtfulness and kindness floods my existence. Always blessed with a really close cohort of deep and meaningful friendships, never before had I the need to lean on and realise the depth and healing of good friends and my close family.

But it doesn't stop there. People I work with, have worked with, knew before and don't even know so well, continuously surprise me with offerings of help, heartfelt wishes, some financial gifts and the list goes on. I am being healed by a community of people who want to ease my pain in any way they can. Too many have suffered or know someone trying to piece back their lives or reinvent themselves in the wake of such tragedy. I am eternally grateful to so many and on an odd occasion, when love floods me, I can for a moment in time even thank him for the learning and gift his act has brought. Even as I write this, I almost cannot believe such a feeling is possible and yet it's true. I can have those moments.

And so, now what? That question remains somewhat unanswered. The time to return to work arrives and I know with certainty that that particular job is no longer for me. So with a deep trust that my life experience is going to provide me with another source of income, I retire. It's the craziest thing in the rational mind to do. My circumstances are dire and yet it feels right on target. I've been tested, tried, turned inside out and upside down. I barely recognise my life now. In eighteen months I have had to let go of all that I spent my lifetime building and have been catapulted into a new existence having to rely on the goodness of others and my own resolve to get by. 'When everything changes, change everything.' For me, this is how it is.

Chapter 22
The next chapter

Despite the range of random acts of kindness, goodness, love and support of people, alongside my efforts to stay positive, within a couple of months it is clearly evident that it is unsustainable for me to continue living under such financial strain. This, coupled with a strong sense of having no ground, swaying like a kite in a hurricane, means that disillusionment sets in and I'm left with little or no sense of purpose. It's as if the tourist visa of my current existence has run out, and it's time for a reality check, a plan. So I ask myself, given the circumstances, 'What do I know in relation to my life currently?'

I know that Ciara has finished college and is making her own way in the world. What I have to offer her she doesn't require right now. I know writing makes sense in some way, as it gives me some semblance of purpose and that's worth its weight in gold to me. I know my relationship is expanding and thriving, and Derek, in the wake of what has happened, is looking to move himself and break out of the mould somehow. I know life as I knew it is unrecognisable and beyond repair. I know there is a certain freedom in having packed up the family home, as I'm no longer a slave to the responsibility to all that house carried. I know a feeling of dread surrounds the next few months as the time of year arrives again. I know that it's time to do something totally different.

Out of this mesh of feelings, facts and confusion decisions are made. Courageous, brave or crazy, Derek and I hatch a plan to go to

Thailand for six months, back to that island I had visited a few months before. I can continue to write and he can get some space from all that has been familiar for the past twenty years and see what unfolds. He puts his house on the market and it sells so quickly that he and his ex barely have time to catch their breath, but it feels like a good omen. My days are now filled with helping him pack up his history to join mine, in boxes in Ruth's shed. Days are busy and laden with jobs. In the meantime, I am researching loan options and possible repayment plans, as it's the only way I can support this idea. It's a far cheaper option than living in Ireland and the loan will last longer. We discuss how we may find work out there. He has been a therapist for the past twenty years and has a reputation of success. Ideas fill our minds and conversations take place about what we will study, how we may design more workshops to run, what work we may find and how life will feel warmer for the next six months at the very least.

I am anxious to be gone before any important dates appear – his birthday, Christmas, his anniversary – all of which feel too heavy to bear. It doesn't escape me that his sister won't have me around for those dates and I sway in and out of strong feelings of guilt. She doesn't express much grief around me and clearly supports me going away. Our relationship is good yet there's a distinct fog around us. A symbiotic need to protect each other making our time together an interactive, practical, enjoyable time, with an elephant in the room that we acknowledge from time to time but don't quite know what to do with. That helpless feeling as a parent who cannot make things better for her is often around me like an annoying fly buzzing in my ear. Guilt and shame that I'm not a success!

As time is moving on, the loss seems to gain a new quality of realness and a depth that is perceptible to my sensitive nature which is somewhat harder to express. It's as if I'm all cried out and so the feeling is underneath a lot of other daily small irritations that when addressed bring me right down into the real feeling. Disbelief that he is gone and he chose that for himself coupled with the idea that I cannot interact with him on a physical level is still so unreal in some way and yet it's my everyday experience for a year and a half now.

The level of guilt and shame in relation to his choice has reached new proportions. We live in a society whereby we are judged by the successes of our offspring. I know this to be true as a parent who, despite a little tinge of sadness, beamed with pride at Ciara's graduation. How then can I hold my head up when I failed so dismally at the most important job in the world with him? He left so young. What does that say about me and his father? With Ciara, even without the extenuating circumstances in her case, this day of honouring her work in getting her degree would fill her dad and me with pride. Our need for our children to make us feel proud is not unlike that of any other parents. How often do we hear someone say, you must be very proud of him or her? And I am so proud of his sister who even in the face of his untimely death managed to continue with her studies and get her degree.

How can a young sixteen-year-old Pakistani woman, who is singled out and shot for speaking out about the injustice of not being allowed to be educated in her society simply because of her gender, not only speak louder but address the UN and inspire the world? Malala Yousafzai turned her atrocity around and made her life a model for courage and transformation. So many young people I worked with in the social care system have such difficult roads to walk, having little or none of the advantages others take for granted, their very fundamental need for safety and shelter not being met. They carry their loads as best they can without the need to end it all. What's the difference in a successful inspiring adult that started with the odds stacked against them? What is it that calls them to rise above their circumstances and show us all what is possible?

What in Darragh was missing that he felt he needed to throw in the towel and leave so abruptly? He grew up without intense difficulties, challenges or abuse in his daily life. Can I even trust now that is true? Is there something he hid from me? The answers lie in a place that I can't access and it's one of the most frustrating outcomes of such an act. These questions can be speculated on for hours, days, weeks at a time!

I can and do move myself out of this thinking whenever possible, as it serves me not. It's what I call 'cul-de-sac thinking', ending up in the same loop of what if? Here I feel forsaken by my belief system, my choices, my God. It results in me wanting to crawl under a blanket and not show my head. Sometimes that blanket feels comforting, enticing me to stay under, but I know I must go on. I am so determined to help myself live in peace with all of this, and anyone else out there too.

And so, I'm in the midst of packing yet again! There is this underlying record playing quietly in the background, one that could take the already shaky ground out from under me if I entertain it too much. The need to find a loan is terrifying. How will I generate enough income to repay it? I feel I'm being asked to trust again when my trust in life is smashed, and I need someone to trust me also that I can repay a loan when I'm not sure anymore that I can be trusted. The feeling is really disconcerting. It's like my feet are on a moving platform in a vast river and I've no rails to hold on to. I don't know where I belong. Clinging on to my relationship like an overhanging branch in the surging swell of tidal waters could drown us both, so being busy and caught up in details is a most welcome distraction. The signs that somehow I'm on the right track do start to become clearer.

A mentor appears for my writing. A shining support, Johnny, a friend of Gregg's, reads my work, gives me feedback and his enthusiasm excites me into feeling a real possibility that these words will mean something to others. A criminologist, his realism a good antidote to my more spiritual orientation. This realism superseded by a dedication and genuine interest in helping people. He becomes a lifeline for me. I secure a loan from my loving friend that will get the ticket and last me at least half of the time. Work is likely in the place we are going to, as therapists flock there.

The time ticks by so quickly while plans are forming and becoming real, and before we know it, the departure date arrives. We are jumping off the cliff so to speak, without the safety harness, into a new chapter of our relationship, our lives as a couple and our working lives. We have burned our bridges, given up the bread-and-butter work. Derek has sold his home and settled matters with his ex while I've rented mine so effectively there's no backup plan. It's all out there in the vortex of possibility. Again the thought doesn't escape us and is voiced by some of our friends and family. 'Are you crazy at your age and stage in life?' I hear from loving parents. Are we courageous pioneers? Brave or stupid? That remains to be seen.

Chapter 23
Eastwards we go

Travelling together is fun and despite long flights in small spaces, we keep it loving and light between us. Waking up in Bangkok to the sound of excited children's voices curiously anticipating meeting the late-arriving guests of the night before is both surreal and sweet.

We are stopping over in a friend of Derek's house. Nestled in a beautiful compound of houses with a lake, this oasis in the city makes for a pretty soft landing. Welcomed and spoilt, we get to explore a thriving Bangkok from a cushioned base. We revel in the heat, the warm welcome and the help to find our way around.

Downtown Bangkok is a bustle of noise, such a vibrancy of activity and life. Loud car horns fill the air as haphazard drivers in colourful traffic share the smog-filled space with tuk-tuks. Open-sided with covered seats, these bike-like vehicles contribute to the noise and smog while meandering through lanes of traffic, adding to the spectacle. Scooters by their hundreds are randomly zigzagging through to find the shortest route. Not a helmet in sight as two, three and even families of four balance precariously on these noisy contraptions. Temples gleaming under the sun, embossed in gold and colourful jewels, glisten in the distance. We are left in no doubt that we are far from home.

Smells assault the senses as street vendors cook on hot flames, shaking the wok-like pan with vegetables, chicken, noodles and all manner of food which beckons the passer-by to sample. Hot and sticky, the atmosphere is intense. Shopping centres sprawling over large spaces are busy with shoppers mooching in bargain rails or pondering over the next designer brand. Heeled and jewelled, young and carefree, tanned and sun-kissed, old and young, transgender, transsexual – people of all walks of life throng the streets in this melting pot of the world.

What the heck are we doing? Are we doing the right thing? I spew questions at Derek a few days later as we repack our new rucksacks for the next part of the trip. He is reassuring in his response. 'This is such an adventure,' he replies. 'Let's look at it that way.'

Our journey and my return to the island is remarkable and terrifying as giant swelling waves have all but one brave boatman grounded. The last lap of the journey is in a long-poled, engine-propelled rowboat. I am really unsure of the wisdom of entering the waters at all. Before I can change my mind, however, we have clambered ungraciously aboard as the boat bobs frantically in the swell – only us and the two boatmen. This is not how I recalled my last visit. What has happened to the tropical blue-green flat waters and boats laden with people swaying back and forth, sailing around the headland to the beaches on the other side?

I'm committed now, there's no escape. We are at the mercy of the raging waves, the skill of this man at the helm and that long pole. It's both terrifying and exhilarating; a bit like a metaphor for this whole journey. Staying inside the boat becomes the focus, holding on as we rise up and crash back down time after time. Inside I'm hovering between terror and excitement much like the rise and fall of the large swell. Derek is totally thrilled by it all. I can see he is loving the edginess and adrenalin rush. Drenched by salt water, every moment feels lengthened, and as we round the headland I am relieved to see the beach off in the distance, except we are not remotely turning in that direction.

I turn to look at the boatman questioningly. He is totally focussed and almost in a trance as he navigates the next wave. We cannot land there as it is too precarious to navigate, and so we continue to the next bay. There's nothing to do but hang on and expect we will make it; another apt metaphor for my life. After what seems like a lifelong journey, we finally get to a beach, get our shaky wet selves and our luggage off the boat and bid the boatman farewell as he turns the boat around. So our initiation to the jungle island feels a little different than my last time, but intensity is a common theme.

The swarm of dragonflies over our heads I take to be a good omen. A long-standing emblem of mine, I love their capacity to defy gravity and fly with their large bodies and fragile wings. Despite the weight of the burden I carry I'm still looking to fly.

We have a long trek over the jungle hill and at least I know this time to leave a heavy bag against a rock and come back for it when one load has made the journey. I am both surprised and delighted when various members of staff remember me from before and I feel welcome. It makes sense of the decision to return to the place I had been living on my own some months earlier. We are shown to our new home, our first together as a pair. The jungle hut, one of those placed high on a hill cocooned in the leafy plants of the jungle, is musty and old; but its privacy and view more than compensate.

The next few days continue with a mix of awe and tension. Stormy weather is both fascinating and sleep-interrupting, as loud thunder bursts overhead. A feeling of exposure as the little cabin of bamboo seems barely able to sustain its form in the din. A bat chasing a dragonfly around the light on our little porch is such a joy to witness whilst we duck in response to the quick flying of the bat. The wind blows the dark clouds from the night sky, exposing the bejewelled prizes glittering beneath. Nature in its raw potent power is so paradoxical. Fear and awe, often in the same fragment of a second, are cast in an ever-changing cauldron of experiences: this majesty of greenery, sitting on top of the steep mountainous incline with most of the inner core of the island too steep to house any human activity.

Because things are not like I remembered them from only months earlier, it makes me feel unsettled. Derek and I seem to be drifting in and out of total connection and intimacy to that space where a perceptible gap is between us and communication is skirting over the top of things. But discerning what those things are is posing a challenge. I am expectant and wait for the feeling of me that emerged before in this environment to emerge. So far, there is no sign of it. Derek is wrestling with his own adjustment issues. He had a hectic preparation for leaving life behind to come here to a place where there are no demands on time, and he is struggling to make sense of the contrast. Also, the mosquitoes discover a newcomer and devour him, testing his resolve even more as lumpy, painful, itchy bumps arise in dispute on his skin.

Meanwhile, the beach heaves with very beautiful bikini-clad women parading in front of us, some hula-hooping with the style and tenacity worthy of a circus, others practising yoga or dance techniques by the water's edge. Most are young, beautiful and toned.

This makes me feel a bit unsure of myself, middle-aged, hardly toned, and the lack of a mirror seems almost like a blessing. I catch the vanity of this, reminding myself I have bigger fish to fry. The wondering at the madness of our decision gets louder and more demanding. Are we insane? How in the world am I to live now? How are we to make our way? Will the 'us' we are now thrive or struggle with these new points of reference that don't resemble life to date? We in our middle years with the security others take for granted gone and we choosing to let it all go. Security! As if such a thing exists! People, relationships, material things all surround us and we hold them tight to help us feel secure and comforted. Some operate tight control in routine and the scheduling of themselves and their loved ones to create a strong feeling of security. But as my beloved son showed me, it's a house of cards that can be blown down in a second. Nonetheless, this big break to the jungle and flying without a parachute is feeling rather silly and irresponsible.

As days melt into weeks, our experiences continue to bring a mixture of tension and relaxation. The place we live is a small community and we meet people on a daily basis in the confined area of three small bays. Finding space, finding purpose and letting go of a familiar framework are all bearing down on us. Yahtri the Swiss jungle trekker is back, and he and Derek strike up a close friendship on their expeditions across the mountain. We do OK, we check in, we use the processes and tools we have learned over the years but paradise is paradoxical. Even the waters wash up so much garbage on the beach it can be so difficult to witness and attempts to clean seem futile as the waves bring more. The beauty of nature accosted by human insensitivity, even this begins to become a challenge to observe. Was this the same place I had been just months before? Is selling up shop the reason this feels so different now?

As days turn into weeks, guilt assails me as I feel selfish leaving Ciara in Ireland to meet Darragh's dates, his birthday, anniversary and Christmas. Knowing that she is well-supported by many family and friends, not to mention Kevin and his family, brings but a small relief. I'm her mother and I'm off on the other side of the world. My physical body is struggling also. There is a tension in my upper chest, like a knot in my higher stomach. It's almost as if my heart is tightly bound. My arm and shoulder go into painful spasms, adding to the sleep interruptions already provided by the weather. In this chilled out world, it's as if my body has coiled into a spiral of stress. I am consistently grateful that my therapist-partner can do some work to relieve my discomfort and pain, but I'm in regular need of his help.

Thus waking up in paradise is often etched with grumpiness, and I am in need of a lot of self-talk and taking time to appreciate nature, to feel any semblance of well-being. I've been feeling nauseous for a few mornings in the run up to what would be Darragh's seventeenth birthday, and while joking about the usual cause of such symptoms, such as pregnancy, it dawns on me this could be another physiological message my body is producing, like last year's menstruation on his birthday. It seems far-fetched but I don't discount the possibility. In fact as I feel a wave of nausea, under each one is a wave of emotion that I no longer find easy to let out. Is this what it is like for people who find it difficult to really express their feelings? My frustration with this new non-expression is palpable and an emotion in itself.

Our daily breakfast routine takes place in the little restaurant that is part of our hut complex. The variety of food is a surprise to me. Breakfast normally consists of a fruit feast, but cornflakes and milk are also on the menu now tailored to Western needs. Our cabin has no cooking facilities and when we arrive at the restaurant on the day before Darragh's birthday, the music playing stops me in my tracks. It's Swedish House Mafia: 'Don't you worry, don't you worry child, heaven has a plan for you,' blasts out of the speakers. We are on an island in the Gulf of Thailand. It's enough to send a shaky me over the edge. A walk along the shoreline and salty tears is the best combination to let go into the feelings. This anthem that spontaneously erupts in my head periodically since the night I dreamed of him singing this to me is on the speakers here on an island in Thailand. It's both a blessing and a pain-inducing feeling. The longing to squeeze him and tell him how I miss him is almost unbearable. Comforting as the message is, I wish to see some evidence of that plan that heaven has for me as this one is questionable at times. I take it to be a good omen. After a time standing and watching the waves, I gather myself together enough to return to the breakfast, grateful for sunglasses as they hide a multitude.

Derek and I have planned to spend the next two days on another part of the island. The weekly excursion on a scooter to explore the island is one of our favourite pastimes, and today we are planning to stay over in a slightly better-equipped hut, so luxuries like hot water can be enjoyed. Good Wi-Fi is an essential component, as I need to speak to Ciara on his birthday. We gather ourselves, packing a little overnight backpack, putting all our valuables of an electronic nature into a waterproof bag; experience of the long-pole boat trips has rendered us extra cautious. Big waves take no prisoners and care not for the preciousness of technology. 'I'm ready for a change of scenery on the other side of the island,' I say more to myself than anyone.

Perched on the back of a scooter, I am enthralled as the majestic views are breathtaking. Our little rented scooter pushes up the almost vertical hills, giving us bird's eye views of the magnificent coastline framed by lush mountains, and declines as quickly in twists and turns. An occasional sighting of a monkey running along a wire is a novelty and the whole drive is exhilarating. Somehow too I feel closer to Darragh as I revel in the natural beauty. I see him on the sparkle in the water, in the tropical mountain, in the coastline and in the flowers. And yet the ache inside me is deep and growling to express. Tears drip down my face and the wind dries them. It's a bonus I'm here, totally anonymous, no one has to know I'm teary, not even Derek. Coastline gives way to streets lined with wooden stalls, opulent colourful displays of wares, fruits and vegetables, brightly coloured printed dresses, sarongs and beachwear – an eclectic array to tempt the tourists.

We stop and browse in a local market, smells filling our nostrils and in some instances, causing a heave to the stomach. Sanitation is not so developed and so in the blistering heat, sewage odours can accost your system. Food stalls and hot food vendors seem oblivious to such conflicting smells, as do many locals and tourists milling between the selections of food. We find a spot that seems pleasant to our nostrils and drink a refreshing watermelon shake and nibble on some roasted nuts to keep the hunger at bay.

The morning of his birthday dawns, and my first realisation is that those at home won't be even awake for seven more hours and I'm going alone on this for a time. Is that not why I came away in the first place? That growling need to express is getting louder and feels like a lion's roar building inside me. I've lost my cub and he's not coming back. It feels primal and intense and yet inaccessible. No wail escapes my lips as Derek helps me to try to get to the feeling. The mighty roar I feel welling up is audible only to me on the inside.

Derek heads away to an appointment and I sit in a hammock in an unfamiliar place and write. Now I feel nothing – no pain, no sense of Darragh, no fear – just a kind of numbness. The growling lioness has retreated to a cave somewhere in the depths of me.

Later in the day, I finally get to catch up with Ciara when the time-lapse becomes sociable. She repeats the tradition of the birthday balloon on his grave, this time with her father by her side. I am relieved to hear that she sounds fine as she describes her day. 'I met Dad at the graveside,' she says, 'and it was actually not raining so we stayed a while chatting on the bench under the tree Dad likes, near the grave,' she recounts to me across the miles. 'Then we went for breakfast,' she continues. Dave finds solace at the graveside and tends to spend time there. I can sense he carries the burden of guilt and sadness heavily upon his broad shoulders although we see so little of each other since

Darragh left. It's like we cannot communicate anymore.

Louise has taken the day off work and she and Ciara spend time walking in nature, meeting with my family and having dinner together. I get to speak to a collective group of family on Skype. This miracle of technology, when you have good Wi-Fi, is such an asset at times like this, and we share stories of how we spent his birthday day on opposite sides of the world. It feels OK as I am still in the kind of numbness that doesn't call for feeling.

Time races on and before long it is his anniversary day. Once again the feelings swirl around swelling to the surface but not breaking the film that covers over. It's as if I have lost the capacity to express the pain. This both fascinates and torments me simultaneously.

Once again we have taken a scooter and are off on an adventure of exploration. It seems fitting to do something different on his occasion days. We are in a local town having been stopped in our tracks by a massive monsoon downpour. We meander around under a tarpaulin-covered market where rows and rows of street traders exhibit their clothes and handbags for the tourists to purchase. I am looking absentmindedly at a brightly coloured sarong when I feel a strong tingling on my back and shoulders. I know it's him trying to let me know he is around me. I can almost hear his voice saying, 'Go on Ma, treat yourself.' Derek comes up behind me and knows in an instant what is going on. 'I feel like he wants me to treat you,' he says. 'Let's buy that sarong.' I can only nod in tears as he purchases the sarong and leaves me to gather myself a little. It astounds me that Derek's sensitivity is such that my son comes through him like this to access me. This is not the first or the last time that my son finds a channel through my partner. The feeling of him around me tantalises me now and causes me to yearn once again for his physicality.

I feel a strong urge to contact Ciara with the same message. 'Let yourself be spoiled today,' I text her, suggesting she take money from my account to treat herself to something nice, a gift from her brother. Knowing she will not even be awake yet, I send the message anyway as I feel it's important. The remainder of the day is easy and more relaxed for me than his birthday. It's as if feeling him has soothed me and there's a sense of easing of guilt around me being away from his sister. I feel like he approves of where I am and what I am trying to achieve, even if I am not sure half the time.

And so life in our new world continues to pose conflicting experiences. We enquire, meet and get hired as therapists at one of the wellness and detox centres. This asks of us to stand up and pitch ourselves, give talks to large and small groups and run a meditation group once a week as well as our individual sessions. We both enjoy the opportunity this provides to speak about ourselves and sell our particular skill set. The money at the end of the week feels great and is a total bonus. However, after some time, something unsatisfying begins to emerge. There is a culture of drugs among the population at large and it is beginning to affect us. I feel a great sensitivity to that energy and discover that not only clients but some therapists are partaking on a regular basis. It's none of my business generally, and I don't tend to make judgements, but this whole scene unnerves me and I can feel it intensely. It generates a feeling of unsafety especially in the arena of healing. It feels to me like it's beginning to spiral out of control. Regular dance parties are frequented by so many and it becomes the topic of conversation the day after with almost a prize given to those who stay on the dance floor the longest and latest and who is on what stimulant or mood enhancer. It becomes nauseating to me.

Some of these people, it seems, are in search of deeper meaning and an altered perception. Many speak of love and inter-connectedness, crossing into another dimension of reality, that same feeling I recognise from some meditations, communications with Darragh and group experiences but without the drugs. Understanding our innate search as humans to connect to something greater than ourselves, we can choose our paths to achieve that end. Some find it in ritual and religion, some discover it in drugs – an instantaneous, quick and almost guaranteed access to a heightened sensitivity that can lead to an insatiable need for more – and others find it in nature and love and inside themselves. Whatever that drive, it seems to exist in all of us.

We experience many people as they journey on some drug or

other, sometimes all loved up, sometimes tripping out trying to escape some inner demons. Whatever the experiences and choices made by individuals and small groups collectively, it's just not our gig. Derek is feeling the same and we make the tough decision to quit the work, tough for me because I need the finances. It feels like a matter of integrity; I cannot sell my soul for the sake of money, even if it is in a well-intentioned space of healing. We have a really frank discussion with the captain of that particular ship. She is empathic and tells us that she is trying to clean up the situation. She doesn't condone or encourage drug use and for the most part her team are dedicated and responsible. This may all be true but for us, we have a strong sense that we are not a match for this place. We are left now wondering about staying on in this island for the foreseeable future. We left our home with all our eggs arranged in this basket and now it's looking like they are beginning to crack. James, the sweets man, is coming for his Christmas holidays and we decide not to make our decision until after his departure. Once again, the big break to paradise not turning out as expected.

Chapter 24
The island of the moon

We are sitting up on the platform at one of my favourite places to eat. A wooden deck, high on a rock, under the stars! The young Burmese waiter comes to take our order, scaling the rock as if he was born running up and down rocks. 'I am so tired,' he says when he reaches us and as we are indecisive about what to eat he lies down beside me on the deck cloaked by the darkness so his boss cannot see him. We suggest he takes his time as we can keep an eye out for his boss. He tells me he is sixteen and is here working to send money home to his mother. His father died when he was younger and his mother has no money and is getting older.

As he lies there, star and moon gazing, he relates in his broken English the pain he feels at not seeing his mother and how he sometimes cries after they speak on the phone. My heart is gaping open as I know his pain but from the other side: the mother aching for her son. Under the full moon in a starlit sky, he describes his mother. 'She like the moon, she like the sky, she like the stars, I loves her, I really love her,' he says as if under a trance. I am spellbound and can barely breathe listening to this beautiful acknowledgement of his mother flow from him. And here in the darkness under a full moon, he, his mother, my son and I are all joined in a moment of pure magic as tears drop on his cheeks and mine. And then it's done. In typical teenage fashion he sits up, grins at me and says, 'You make up your mind yet what to order?' Derek and Yahtri are as mystified as I am at what has just transpired. They were aware of the whole conversation. This magical moment on this island of the moon is more potent than usual for me. The next day when that same waiter greets us he calls us 'father' and 'mother' and tells us we can be that for him while we are in Thailand. We are suitably touched by this honour he has bestowed upon us.

The beauty of sitting out under the stars on a warm evening for dinner is a constant joy and pleasure to behold. As I watch the moonlit waters break at the shoreline and regularly observe nature in all her glory and majesty, I sometimes imagine that Darragh is part of this greater picture now. I see him flying over the mountain in the eagle; I see him in the sparkles of light on the water. Whenever it is possible, I can and do indulge this thinking and imagining as I bring him closer it seems, even if just for a second.

We are trying to return to our bay one evening but the waves are too high, so we find the only available place to stay. It's called 'Tommy's' – the same name as his joined-at-the-hip friend – and I know he is around as we smile at the check-in desk. Experiences here are somewhat heightened, both positive and negative ones, although I realise that the quality of an experience is dependent upon the relevance or focus we give it. None the less, this tropical existence throws up so many intense moments.

For example, we are returning across the jungle pathway after giving a presentation of our way of working to an audience of therapists and new people arriving on the island. Suddenly in our path, a snake launches forward, his upwards-inclined head and neck fans out and he is hissing. Derek hears the hissing before he sees it and beckons me to run. I don't need much prompting as I am right beside him, and seeing with my own eyes is enough to warrant a getaway response.

It transpires we met a king cobra, an unusual sighting but not the first in these parts. Interestingly the aftermath of such an episode is more telling and longstanding in that a walk I relish for its magnificent views and jungle feel, which is so different to that of the Western world, is now filled with angst and trepidation. Loud rustling anywhere pumps my adrenals and the same with Derek. We find ourselves jumpy on the pathway, using a stick to beat the ground as is recommended.

Another time, we are sitting in the back of a pickup truck, on a bench seat, squashed between people. We stop to pick up a couple of locals left with standing room only, in an already overly packed truck. The air is thick with heat and smells of foliage. The road is a ravine carved out by water through the mountain and the trip feels like a roller coaster ride. As we fall into and on top of each other whilst gripping the bar with all our might in the open back of the pickup, I hear a voice in my head saying, 'Breathe Ma, enjoy the ride!' Again I know it's Darragh by the crystal quality of feeling that fills me. As I exhale I realise I was holding my breath in total tension as we scaled up and skidded down hills in the thick jungle air. Thai men hold the rail in front of me for dear life as they speak incessantly in a language that now sounds familiar but holds no meaning for me. The gasps as people fall on to each other, as the truck again tilts excessively up or downhill, the jungle sounds, the big tyres spinning in the dirt. Suddenly I want to laugh out loud and enjoy the whole spectacle. It feels alive and exciting. Exhilaration floods me and I revel in it, again grateful for the moment of connection with something greater than me.

In the weeks building up to Christmas, my days are filled with writing, resting and wrestling with sleep as my body still seems overrun with adrenalin. A hammock I'm resting in collapses, bringing me to the hard sand on my coccyx. Following this, two days later, I trip over a rock in the darkness on the beach. With only a torch in hand I find my walk to the restaurant almost unbearable. Thankfully, the nature of these places is that people lie or sit at low tables on the floor. So I lie on the cushions and Derek does some miraculous bodywork which, in just a few minutes, renders me able to sit, eat and walk home with relative ease. A week or so later, it's Christmas Eve and we are in a café on the more developed side of the island. A Christmas carol comes over the speaker and we are stunned to realise we have heard no songs, done no shopping, seen no decorations and have had no participation in any of the madness of Christmas. A wave of teary relief floods through me as I recall last year's episode of the tree and the frightening experience of my body barely functioning.

This year the morning dawns warm and sunny, and my playful, bald partner wears a black, curly wig to breakfast to the sheer delight of the staff who are busy decorating the place for the day's festivities.

The young Burmese wait on us hand and foot all day with cheery smiles and helpful attitudes, and we are forming bonds with some of them quickly. My feelings are tame and I can relax into the playful mood shared by us and the staff and our visiting friend. It feels rather novel to be sitting under the coconut trees by the water, and the common tone of the wider group is one of relief not to be caught up in the Western traditions. Of course for those who do like to partake, some of the restaurants have a dinner and Christmas show which we decline. Instead, we attend a buffet, free to all, supplied by our own team, and the feeling is relaxed and communal.

Tables are rearranged into a big square in the centre of the room. Chairs line the low walls of the windowless wooden structure. Staff dressed in their finery pose for pictures with us having filled tables with pots and plates of traditional Burmese and Thai food, rice being the most consistent ingredient. It is such an eclectic group of people – from Australia to Canada, Ireland, Russia and many more – each with their own story of the life they have lived to date; each with their own beliefs about how life should be. We each now share this space, this food and these experiences on a small island in the Gulf of Thailand. How wonderful and unexpected is this outcome for me, for us! Our visiting friend, James, is completely captivated by the incredible experience.

But it is calls home that must take precedence over all else. I am relieved once again to find Ciara is good and spending the day with Dave and her younger brother, Cillian. His five-year-old presence, she says, makes Christmas feel pleasant for her, as he pulls her to play with his new toys in sheer delight and wonder.

Sleep continues to pose a problem in the intervening days between Christmas and New Year, now for Derek as well as me. A very loud scratching at our heads behind the flimsy mosquito screen is getting progressively louder each night. We turn ourselves around in the bed for two nights at least, putting some distance between our ears and these noises. Geckos are common and we wonder how these newcomers are so much louder than the usual inhabitants. The third night in and a thud in the bathroom jolts me awake. Upon investigation, we find the lid is off the bin, and we are confused by this. Our confusion ends on the night before New Year's Eve when I meet a rat in the very small toilet space.

I hastily close the door and Derek is ready to take action and usher him back out the pipe through which he entered. After a lot of noise, the blood returns to my veins and we settle back to sleep, except now the intense window scratching begins in earnest again. This time we look to see no gecko but another rat. Two rats in one night either end of our little cabin. I sit up and fret, as each time Derek bangs the window the rat returns minutes later. Anxiety turns to anger and frustration at his persistence.

Trapped by rodents on each side of our tiny space, we wonder what the message is for us. Here we are, sitting on the little mosquito-netted bed, on an island, in the midst of our rat debacle. We explore all variables from getting over ourselves, it is a jungle after all, to wondering if we are in the right place at all. It is amazing the possibilities we covered whilst sleep deprived and rat evading. 'What kind of madness is this?' we ask each other intermittently, as the night goes on. Somehow selling up shop at home does not feel like it is playing out so well. We do come to a decision that we are ready to move as soon as James returns home to Ireland. Bali, Burma and Malaysia are all possible as soon as we have researched visas, travel expenses and possible work options.

The dawn of New Year's Eve and two weary, rodent-wildlife adventurers arrive to meet James for breakfast. 'What happened to you two?' he exclaims, 'You look like you have been dragged through a hedge backwards.' He is bemused by our account of our night time escapades and makes a note to be more vigilant around his cabin. As midnight arrives, we watch the fireworks light the beach and water in their noisy colourful explosions. Awe for the spectacle fills me, as rainbow patterns burst out of the smoky noise, splashing lights across the sky that are reflected on the water. I wonder what the animals of the wild make of our noisy human existence. 'Happy New Year,' I whisper to Darragh from deep inside. 'I miss you and long for you still. You better be looking out for your sister, and some guidance for your Ma and Derek wouldn't go astray either.'

I am relieved now, as I have survived the annual required festivities, and this year in better shape than last, a pattern I hope will continue. New Year's Day follows a similar format to Christmas, with young people sitting around discussing parties and last night's activities, none of which we regret missing. Most of them settle on the beach for some sun. I'm missing him so much more this day and wishing he could have stayed alive and travelled like the young people I see all around me. I lean in and ask Derek if he thinks Darragh would have looked like one of the young guys we know if he had lived. This guy seems to have such a look of Darragh and a personality to match that so reminds me of him. It takes a moment or two for Derek to respond and when he does his eyes are filled with tears.

Then he exclaims, 'You have no idea how beautiful he is now, how expansive and alive and rich he is now.' I know it's a moment of precious connection and I allow myself open up to the feeling. It's magical. It's as if the vista we are looking at is somewhat distanced from me yet crystal clear. I look at the people I've got to know here with a greater love than I can express and the same feels true for those I have not made acquaintance with yet. Derek gets a song in his head and plugs the iPod into my ears. It's a song neither he nor I ever listen to usually and the words are so beautiful and poignant. Words that say we were only ever to be together for a short time, goodbye was always to be part of our experience and that love goes way beyond the physical.

It's him, my son Darragh. From across the divide, he is speaking through song to me as I'm sitting on a sun lounger in a land of sunshine and bikinis, people laughing, swimming, relaxing, whilst tears are cascading down my face. It's a beauty as exquisite as the pain gnawing at me. Whatever the explanation, I revel in the glorious feeling of a greater love and connection for as long as it lasts. Twenty minutes or two, it's hard to quantify and makes the first day of the new year memorable. 'Thank you,' I whisper to him. Somehow I know he is keeping an eye on things. Wherever we move to, he will be along for the ride.